THE FROZEN WORLD

ALDUS ENCYCLOPEDIA OF DISCOVERY AND EXPLORATION

Aldus Books London

THE FROZEN WORLD

BY THAYER WILLIS

Executive coordinators: Beppie Harrison
John Mason
Design director: Guenther Radtke
Editorial: Lee Bennett
Damian Grint
Picture Editor: Peter Cook
Research: Elizabeth Lake
Cartography by Geographical Projects

SBN: 490 00233 1
© 1971 Aldus Books Limited, London
First published in the United Kingdom
1971 by Aldus Books Limited,
17 Conway Street, London, W.1.
Printed in Yugoslavia by
Mladinska Knjiga, Ljubljana.

Contents

Left: signpost at the Geographic South Pole, situated in the coldest and most desolate region on earth. It was not until 1911 that the first explorers reached this strange, feature-less point on the continent from which the only direction is north.

Frontispiece: the crewmen of Willem Barents' expedition to the Arctic in 1596 shooting a polar bear. Their desperate attempt to hack a path for their ship, caught fast in the ice, to the open water was unsuccessful, and they had to winter in the Arctic.

List of Maps

The two illuminated globes show the Arctic (left) and the Antarctic as they would appear from a point immediately above the North and South poles respectively. The Arctic is a frozen sea that lies between the continents of Asia (top) and North America. Antarctica is a vast frozen continent, about the size of Africa north of the equator, between South America (top) and Australasia.

The Ends of the Earth

1

By mid-morning on April 6, 1909, a United States naval officer, Robert E. Peary, accompanied by his Negro servant and four Eskimos, had reached a position on the ice that they estimated to be just three miles south of the North Pole. Although they were only a few miles from their goal, both the men and their dogs were too exhausted to continue. After 20 years of Arctic exploration and the last 12 years trying to reach the pole, Peary was on the brink of success. But he was too tired to realize that his life's purpose had almost been achieved. The accumulated weariness of six days and nights of forced marches and the constant anxiety of the journey seemed to roll across him. As soon as the Eskimos had constructed *igloos* (snow houses) for everyone, and the men had eaten and given a double ration to the dogs, Peary crawled into his igloo for a few hours' rest.

Weary though he was, Robert Peary could not sleep for long.

Left: men and dogs in the remote icy expanses at the ends of the earth, still the most successful combination for polar journeys. Here the dog teams of the transarctic expedition led by Wally Herbert in the winter of 1968–1969 cross the endless Arctic ice fields.

Right: Commander Robert E. Peary, the first man to reach the North Pole. Peary said, "The arctic brings a man face to face with himself. If he is a man, the man comes out; and if he is a cur, the cur shows as quickly."

Above: icebergs and pack ice float in the ghostly desolation of the ocean surrounding the frozen continent of Antarctica. The polar regions have a haunting, austere beauty that has proved irresistible to many explorers.

When he awoke a few hours later, he picked up his diary and wrote these words: "The Pole at last! I cannot bring myself to realize it. It seems all so simple and commonplace."

Then Peary and two Eskimos loaded some food and navigation instruments aboard a sledge and pushed on northward for about 10 miles to a position beyond the pole. After a march of only a few hours, Robert Peary became the first man to actually stand at the North Pole the summit of the world. There was nothing there to mark the magical point—that invisible spot on the Arctic ice where the directions of east, west, and north disappear and only one direction remains—south.

The following day the small party of six men turned their sledges toward the south and began to race toward the northern coast of Ellesmere Island and their ship that was waiting at Cape Columbia.

Peary knew that if they were to reach land again they would have to hurry. What worried him most was the possibility of a gale that could break up the ice over which they traveled. Once broken the *floes*, or floating sheets of ice, would become separated by *leads*, or areas of open water. The breaking up could in turn speed up the drift of the ice eastward in the direction of the tepid North Atlantic. The comparative warmth of the water in that region would melt the solid ice from beneath them. The safe return of Peary and his companions to Cape Columbia 16 days later ended one of the greatest success stories of man against the elements.

Peary's triumph in overcoming the problems of getting to and from the North Pole tells us a great deal about the Arctic. First of all, there is the region of continuous cold around the North Pole. Here, there is no land, just a solid surface of ice in the midst of the Arctic Ocean. In his earlier travels Peary had been to, or very near, the other parts of the Arctic. These include the Arctic Ocean and its thousands of islands, and the northern parts of the continents of Europe, Asia, and North America.

Like every explorer who has tried to get to the North Pole, Peary had to leave land behind him and travel over the ice. Moreover, he had to do this at the coldest and darkest time of the year when the ice was firm and no open water barred his way. He also had to contend with the drift of the ice that is always moving. This meant that Peary had to allow for this drift in setting his course northward. There was also the difficulty of establishing supply depots along the route. A cache of food left at a particular spot on the march northward would not be at that spot when the expedition returned south. The drifting pack ice was again the explanation for this. Even if he took the chance of locating a supply of food he had left behind several weeks before, he still faced the risk of finding that it had been raided by foxes or polar bears in the meantime.

The first European known to have ventured into the Arctic region was Pytheas, a Greek mathematician and explorer. In 325 B.C., he sailed around Britain and headed north in search of a land

Right: part of the *Carta Marina* drawn by the Swedish bishop Olaus Magnus (1490–1558), showing Iceland and Greenland—the first map to give an accurate picture of the far north.

Above: a bronze Viking plaque of the 600's, showing two bears attacking a man. Greenland, where Eric the Red established his colonies, had a milder climate than it has today, and Viking settlers were able to grow vegetables and feed their stock in pastures in the summer. Even during the winter they could hunt the animals that roamed the wild areas beyond the settlements.

called Thule (which may have been Norway or Iceland), which he had learned about from the Britons. For hundreds of years, however, no one believed Pytheas' story or his description of the continuous daylight that occurs around the area from May through July. Europeans, and in particular the Romans, thought that ice covered everything in the north and that no ships could travel there.

About 300 years after the Roman Empire had lost its influence in the world (during the A.D. 400's) Europeans again began to sail north to the Arctic. The first to do so were Christian monks from Ireland. They were looking for a place of solitude as they sailed in their small, open, round-bottomed boats and followed the path of migrating geese to Iceland. The date of their arrival there was about 770. A hundred years later the first Norsemen, or Vikings, reached Iceland to settle there. These were bands of Scandinavian sea rovers who were the ancestors of today's Norwegians, Swedes, and Danes.

Then about the year 900, a Norseman named Gunnbjørn was blown off course on his way to Iceland. After drifting for days through the dangerous Arctic waters he at last sighted land—the black, ice-studded cliffs of east Greenland. When the storm finally abated, he made his way back to Iceland with stories of a new land that lay six days' sail to the west.

The adventurous Vikings were excited by the tale. They had

already colonized Iceland and were now eager to find new lands. Still, it was a risky voyage and Gunnbjørn's descriptions of drifting ice and dense fog soon damped their enthusiasm. About 82 years passed before a Norseman set out with some companions to retrace Gunnbjørn's westward voyage. This was Eric the Red. After he first sighted the east coast of the island Gunnbjørn had seen, he sailed around the dangerous belt of icebergs that hugged the coast. Eric then rounded the southern tip of the island and landed near the present-day port of Eriksey at the entrance to Eriksfjord.

Much of the new land he saw looked like Iceland: rocky islets covered with seabirds, deep fiords cutting into the coastline, an abundance of seals, fish, and whales. Inland, at the protected heads of the fiords, Eric found grassy meadows and hills, dotted with dwarf-juniper and willow trees. In the summer it was warm enough to raise vegetables and there was plenty of pastureland. Along the coast Eric and his companions found the fishing excellent. Seals and walruses were also numerous and provided both food and clothing.

From the time of Eric until the early 1900's, Greenland became much colder, and today most of this largest island in the world is covered by ice. But with the exception of Greenland, explorers and scientists have found that in summer nine-tenths of all Arctic lands have no snow and ice. Berries, vegetables, and a large variety of

Above: the problems of taking ships to the polar regions are as difficult today as they were for the earlier explorers. Here the U.S.S. *Atka* lies at McMurdo Sound, Antarctica. In both Arctic and Antarctic waters ships can quickly become locked in the ice.

13

Above: the crosier of a Viking bishop, found in a Greenland grave, probably that of Jon Smyrill (which means "sparrow-hawk"), who died in 1209. It was during the 900's that the Viking colonies in remote Greenland were converted to the Christian faith.

Opposite: a map of the world from a psalter of the 1200's, showing it as a flat disk with the holy city of Jerusalem at the center. It was believed that an impassable ocean lay encircling the disk, which long discouraged exploration into the seas around Europe.

flowers grow along the North American coast, northern Siberia, and the northernmost parts of Norway, Sweden, and Finland. During the winter the sun never shines on much of the Arctic. But in some Arctic regions it shines at midnight at certain times in the summer. This phenomenon, known as the midnight sun, occurs at the Arctic Circle on June 22, and farther north the periods of midnight sun last longer. For example in northern Norway there is continuous daylight from May through July.

Many of the animals that Eric the Red saw on Greenland in 982 still roam the Arctic. The reindeer and the caribou are the most common, and they generally come in great herds to the summer pasturelands. Bears, foxes, hares, and squirrels also provide both food and fur for the people living in the Arctic. Three species of seals live year-round in Arctic waters, and they are joined by herds of walruses, and schools of belugas and narwhals. Arctic *char* (a variety of trout) choke the far northern rivers and streams in spring, when they return to spawn. In the ocean off the coasts of North America, Siberia, and the Scandinavian countries there are halibut, salmon, and above all cod. To those skilled in hunting and fishing the north supplied almost everything needed for life.

In the summer of 985 about 500 Icelanders followed Eric the Red to the wonderful island to the west that he called Greenland. Most of them established villages around the fiords along the milder southwestern coast, the first colony being in the region of the present-day port of Julianehab.

Word of their successful landing on Greenland reached Iceland and eventually Norway. Other emigrants began to risk the cold and stormy journey by open boat to join the colonists on Greenland. Many people built farms for themselves out of stone and peat, and generally the settlers appear to have flourished in their new home-land. In the summer they farmed, and during the winter months kept themselves supplied with food and clothes by fishing and hunting. According to ancient Norse records, it was not long before the Greenlanders began trading with the Eskimos, exchanging their corn and the iron they imported from Norway for ivory walrus tusks and the skins of bears and seals that the Eskimos had for sale.

Christianity was already established in Greenland by the 1100's, when a bishop was sent to the island to preside over the religious life. The Norwegian Vikings, by paying taxes, even helped to finance the early crusaders to liberate the Holy Land.

In 1261, the Greenlanders voted to become a crown colony of Norway. But by this time their prosperity was beginning to decline. The mild climate that had made farming possible in both Green-land and Iceland was changing. As temperatures dropped, ice began to cover more of the land. At the same time fewer Norwegian ships came to Greenland because of a depressed economy in Norway.

The Greenlanders had relied completely on Norway for their supplies of iron tools, salt, and other necessities. By the middle of the 1300's years would pass without the arrival of a single ship from the

mother country. According to the evidence found by archaeologists the Norse colonies in Greenland seem to have died out in the 1400's. Bodies that have since been found show signs of starvation and scars from wounds. Perhaps when the economy declined and food became scarce, war broke out between the Greenlanders and the Eskimos. Because no records survived to give us a clue to their fate, no one really knows what happened to them.

In the second half of the 1200's, long before the Greenlanders vanished, Europe had been dazzled by the tales brought back by Marco Polo of the fabulous wealth of the Orient—the East Indies, China, and Japan. But the overland routes that Polo had followed were closed to the Christians by the Moslems whose empire, from about 750 to the 1200's, had extended from the Atlantic Ocean to the borders of India. Thus the rich profusion of Oriental silks, spices, tapestries, porcelain, and precious stones were protected—at least for a while. In the early Middle Ages many people in Western Europe

Above: a world map by a French cartographer, Guillaume Le Testu, for a 1555 atlas. It shows a globe cut in two, pulled open, and printed inside and out. Like most early maps, it is based mainly on supposition, but Le Testu's concept of polar geography is amazingly accurate. The Arctic (at left) is an icy sea, and Antarctica is a land mass.

Right: an Indian miniature of a European sailor. During the rush of exploration that began during the 1400's sailors from Europe probed the far reaches of the world, searching for a way to the famous wealth of the East. Their long journeys disproved the myths that frightened the medieval Europeans.

still believed that the earth was a flat disk centered on Jerusalem, and surrounded by a continuous and impassable ocean. They thought it was impossible to sail to the East. Gradually in the 1400's the idea that the earth was round began to be accepted by educated people. At this time the theories and observations of the Greek geographer and astronomer Ptolemy (who had lived in Alexandria, Egypt in about A.D. 150) were translated into Latin, the language used by most educated men. His eight-book *Geography* contained lists of latitude and longitude that provided mapmakers with a system of showing where a place existed on the globe. By the late 1400's the earth was thought of as a globe and divided into equal parts, the lines of longitude running north and south along the earth's surface, and those of latitude running around the earth parallel to the equator. Maps began to look like the maps of today, and explorers began to think of circumnavigating the earth.

In his *Geography* Ptolemy had also written about a vast land to the south that joined Africa and Asia together and stretched across the bottom of the world. For many hundreds of years this great unknown southern land, *Terra Australis Incognita* (unknown south land), was the setting for numerous frightening myths. Here was a place of ghosts where only Satan could feel at home, bounded on the north by terrific heat and in the south by bitter cold. A map made in the 1300's shows pictures of the terrible inhabitants that lived there. The Antarctic Ocean was thought by many sea captains to be a place of towering waves from which the hand of the Devil reached out to snatch at unwary ships.

Then in the 1400's seamen sailing under the rival flags of Spain and Portugal began to dispel these myths. As they made their way around the southern tip of Africa, they disproved the ancient theory that Africa was linked with a third continent to the south. Then Ferdinand Magellan on the first voyage around the world (1519–1521) saw, beyond the strait that bears his name, a land he called Tierra del Fuego (land of fire). This new land was soon included on maps as the northern tip of a continent. Magellan thought it was a group of islands, but as the years went by other seamen and geographers began to put Tierra del Fuego on maps as the northern tip of a vast Antarctic continent separated by the Strait of Magellan from the mainland of South America. For the next 200 years the idea of a fertile Southern Continent was the subject of speculation.

It was not until the late 1700's that men such as Captain James Cook actually set out to look for the mysterious land. Between 1800 and 1820, American and British seal hunters sighted islands around Antarctica, primarily about the area of the South Shetland Islands. One of the men, Nathaniel B. Palmer, from Stonington, Connecticut, may have been the first man to actually see the Antarctic Peninsula. When he returned from his search for fresh seal hunting grounds south of Deception Island he had a rather gloomy story to tell. He had sailed along the coast of "an extensive mountain

Above: emperor penguins on Ross Island, Antarctica, one of the varieties found on the Southern Continent. The Adélie penguin is another, named—like Adelie Land—for the wife of the French explorer Dumont d'Urville.

country, more sterile and dismal if possible and more heavily laden with ice and snow than the South Shetlands."

Explorers began to take an interest in the forbidding, storm-swept land during the 1800's. But it was not until the 1900's that anyone penetrated well into the frozen white wilderness that covers an area of about 5,100,000 square miles across the bottom of the world. Men like Robert Falcon Scott, Sir Ernest Shackleton, and Sir Douglas Mawson were among the first to give an accurate picture of this fifth largest continent on earth. They experienced the hurricane-force winds that scream across the Antarctic—winds that drive snow before them at speeds of up to 200 miles an hour. They suffered the agony of frost-bitten toes and hands when temperatures drop to around −40°F. along the coasts. Some of them even wintered in the Antarctic and managed to stay alive on this icebound continent where inland the mercury plunges sometimes as low as −100°F.

As they made their way from the Ross Ice Shelf, explorers found a range of mountains bordering the vast central plateau. These had to be crossed in order to get to the South Pole. Between the mountain peaks, which ranged from 6,000 to 12,000 feet in height, were great rivers of blue ice that moved slowly down to the sea.

It was a lonely land that these explorers risked their lives to discover. Separated from the nearest mainland by 600 miles of the most tempestuous ocean on earth, they found only a few hardy plants and insects on the rocky mountain sides. Although there were seals, whales, fish, and penguins along the coast, as they struggled inland the explorers were to find no animals to supplement the food they carried with them. Unlike the Arctic where each summer the tundra brightens with scores of plants, only three kinds of flowering plants grow on the Antarctic Peninsula.

For the explorer the difficulties of the Antarctic are great: the frightening temperatures, the physical strain imposed by the high

altitudes in the mountains, the menace of sudden blizzards, and the crevasses formed by slowly shifting ice sheets. Yet, despite these obstacles, it retained its lure.

In the story of exploration Antarctica is unique as the one continent whose real discoverers are known to us. Although we do not know definitely how prehistoric man migrated over the earth's surface, one of the earliest known migrations took place when prehistoric men moved from North Africa to Europe. Gradually people speaking an Indo-European language probably spread throughout Asia. Then, more than 20,000 years ago, men crossed the Bering Strait to North America and eventually worked their way southward into South America. Thus when explorers first reached these continents they had been preceded by Stone Age men. Even the most remote islands of the Pacific, such as Easter Island, were inhabited when the Dutch reached there in 1722. But the explorers and fishermen who first landed on Antarctica were, in fact, the first men to see this frozen world.

Right: the frozen world of the Antarctic is a place where scarcely anything blooms—except here, the Botanical Garden of Wilkes Station. As a relief from his scientific duties during Operation Deep Freeze, the station leader managed to fit a plexiglass dome to the side of the main building and planted vegetables.

A Northern Passage to Cathay

2

European explorers began to think about making voyages to the Arctic during the late 1500's. At that time they were trying to find a Northeast or Northwest Passage to Asia. The interest in finding a sea route to the East was particularly strong in England because of a decline in her trading with France and the Netherlands. An even more important incentive however, was the great wealth that Spanish and Portuguese merchants had acquired from the new trading partners they had discovered in America, India, and especially in China (or Cathay as it was then called by Europeans). London merchants and the ruling monarchs became increasingly

Right: Sir Hugh Willoughby. He set
out with Richard Chancellor, but was
forced to winter on the coast of what
is now Norway, where he and his
men died. When their bodies were
found by some Russian fishermen, his
diary—in which Willoughby writes of
their camp as the Haven of Death—was
recovered. It ends abruptly.

interested in providing financial backing for English explorers who
would search for a new route to the East.

The first question to be settled was the best route to the Orient.
To the northeast, the sea was known to be ice-free as far as the
northern tip of Norway. Even beyond the North Cape, Russian
fishermen were known to take their boats eastward as far as the
Ob River. The northwest route, on the other hand, seemed less
hopeful. In 1497, the Italian navigator John Cabot had sailed the
coast of Newfoundland for England without finding a single
opening in the ice that might lead on to Cathay. Three years later
the two Corte-Real brothers, who sailed under the Spanish flag, could
find no limit to the northward stretching coast of America.

In 1551, "The Mysterie and Campanie of Marchants Adventurers
for the Discoverie of Regions, Dominions, Islands, and Places
unknowen" was founded in London. This company of merchant
adventurers became the center of all activities directed toward the
search for a Northeast Passage. Sir Hugh Willoughby was ap-
pointed by the company to command its first expedition. His pilot-
general, a professional seaman named Richard Chancellor, was one
of the best English navigators of his day. In May, 1553, these two
men set out from Deptford, England on the first of many polar
expeditions marked for tragedy.

A great storm off Norway separated their ships. The *Bona Esper-
anza,* Willoughby's ship, though crippled by the gale, finally made
landfall on the northern coast of Norway, where they were forced
to winter. In 1554 their bodies were found there—they had apparently died of scurvy, a wasting disease caused by faulty diet. This

scourge was to claim the lives of polar explorers until the 1900's.

Meanwhile Richard Chancellor had weathered the storm and sailed his ship into the port of Vardo. There he met some Scottish traders, who tried to dissuade him from his search for a Northeast Passage to Cathay. Chancellor refused to be discouraged by their warnings, and headed his ship eastward again. It was midsummer, the days were long, and Chancellor held his course until he came to a place where there was no night at all, "but a continual light and brightness of the sun shining clearly on a huge and mighty sea."

Below: a map showing "Frobishers Straightes," which was supposed to confirm the discovery in 1576 by Martin Frobisher of a wide clear passage to Cathay, made when he sailed westward from Greenland to what is now Frobisher Bay.

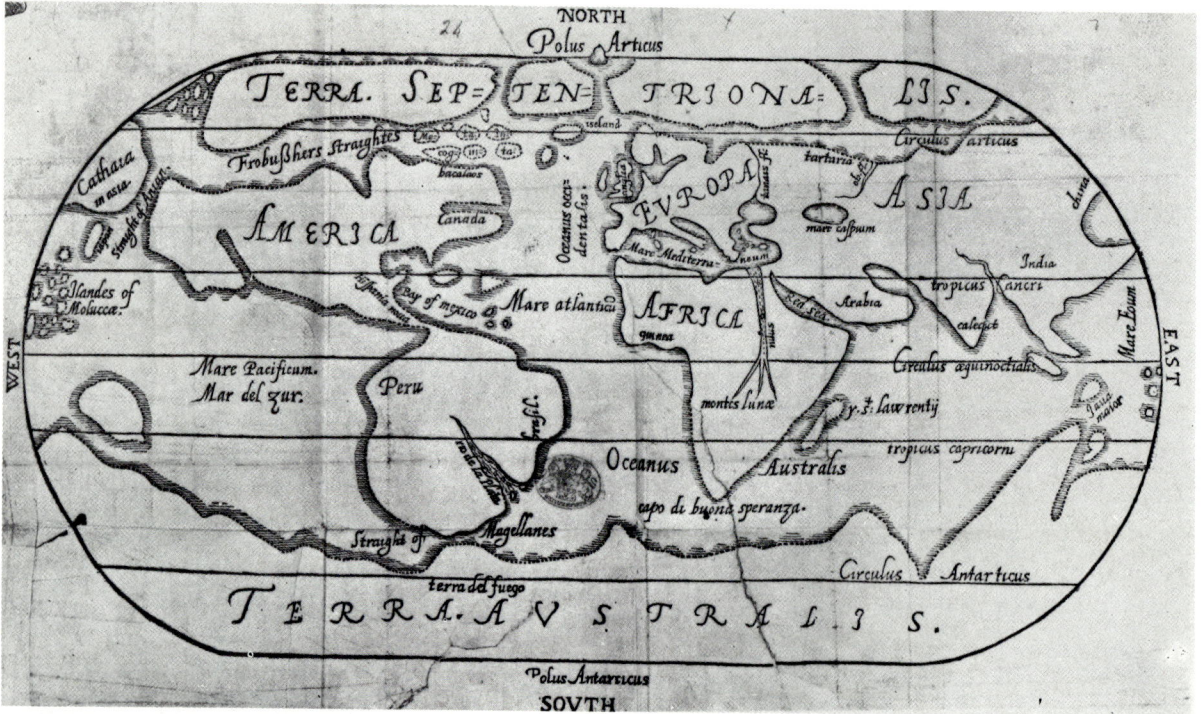

They put into a broad bay, "a hundred miles wide" at the mouth of the Dvina River, near the present-day port of Archangel.

When he went ashore Chancellor was met by emissaries of the Russian czar, Ivan the Terrible. They invited him to accompany them by sledge on the 700-mile journey to Moscow, and Chancellor agreed to do so. When, in the following summer of 1554, he returned to England, Chancellor carried with him a cordial letter from the czar to the King of England. Ivan was hopeful that his greetings would serve to open the way to mutual trade.

Chancellor's voyage led to the formation of the Muscovy Company which, from 1555, developed a lucrative trade with Russia and Persia. The search for a Northeast Passage was thereafter taken over by the Muscovy Company.

Then, during the reign of Queen Elizabeth I, the direction of the

Left: Martin Frobisher. He was convinced that he would find a northern passage to the Pacific like Magellan's southern route. When he sailed in 1576, Queen Elizabeth honored him by waving from her window as his ship sailed by.

search for a route to Cathay was changed to the northwest. In 1569, the publication of Gerhardus Mercator's new map of the world showed that a large land mass in fact blocked the way to the East but that in the West there was the start of a new passage that might lead to Cathay. Arctic exploration was therefore directed westward.

In 1576, the Englishman Sir Martin Frobisher set out from England to look for a Northwest Passage. His expedition, consisting of two small pinnaces, had as its first landfall the southern tip of Greenland. From Greenland he sailed on westward and dis-

Below: an incident from Frobisher's second voyage in 1577, when he made a triumphant return with men to mine the "gold" he found on Baffin Island.

On the map: *Nova Zemla*

Strate de Naſsauwe

Matſlo Delgo

SAMVE TEN LANT

covered Frobisher Bay, an indentation on Baffin Island. As the two ships sailed along the bay Frobisher thought that the land he saw off to the right must be Asia. As they approached the coast of this new land, Frobisher and his men were astonished to see small men in skin-covered canoes paddling toward them. With their Mongoloid features these men were surely inhabitants of the Indies. To prove that he had really reached Cathay Frobisher ordered that one of the Eskimos and a kayak were to be captured and taken in triumph back to London. Frobisher also took back to England some black rocks from Baffin Island that he thought might contain gold.

The return of the expedition to London with the "strange man of Cathay" was a joyful occasion, and Frobisher was treated as a hero. The Eskimo soon died of a cold he had contracted shortly after he arrived in England. But the black rock brought home from Baffin Island seemed to be a more sensational prize. When it was thrown into a fire, it gave off a goldish glow. And rumors of gold were what interested the queen and the merchants of London most. A Cathay Company was formed, gold miners were hastily recruited, and the queen sent Frobisher on another expedition to the Arctic.

On this 1577 voyage Frobisher again landed on Greenland, which he claimed for Queen Elizabeth and named West England. After establishing friendly relations with the Eskimos there, he

Above: the fleet of Willem Barents off Novaya Zemlya, on his first voyage in 1594. Barents was the chief pilot. The fleet was not able to continue farther because the winter was coming on, and so returned to Amsterdam to report on its progress eastward as well as to bring home a walrus.

Above: the exterior of the hut that Barents and his men built on Novaya Zemlya. The illustration shows the events of February 12, 1597, when they were able to shoot a bear from the hut, thus providing not only meat to eat, but also fat to light their lamps during the long dark nights of the winter.

Left: a navigation instrument from Barents' last voyage, discovered in 1871 in the hut that the men had built. Although in ruins, the ice covering it had preserved the objects inside: candlesticks, dishes, even books.

sailed on to Baffin Island for more gold collecting, returning to England as quickly as possible with 200 tons of rock.

His third and last voyage to Baffin Island was the first English colonizing expedition to the Canadian Arctic. There were 15 ships that sailed from London carrying miners to extract more gold, settlers, and a sufficient quantity of supplies for them to build houses and establish a colony on Baffin Island. But no sooner had the fleet entered Frobisher Bay than disaster struck. A storm arose that sent icebergs churning toward the ships. All but a few of them were sunk, thus ending the possibility of establishing a colony on Baffin Island. When Frobisher and the few remaining ships got back to England, they were confronted with even more devastating news. The Baffin ore had after all been wrongly identified as gold—it was nothing more than a worthless mineral called pyrite. Frobisher's claims of having found the Northwest Passage and the frontiers of Cathay were discredited.

In 1585, another English seaman, more modest than Sir Martin Frobisher, was put in charge of an expedition to chart the coasts of "West England" and Baffin Island. This was John Davis who was to make three Arctic voyages during the next three years. He made detailed journeys into the fiords of Greenland and then pushed northward into the unexplored waters of Baffin Bay. But always the

Above: Baffin's route chart of his 1615 voyage, showing by a "red prickle line" his route into Hudson Strait and the mouth of the Foxe Basin. The crosses show the places he landed "to make tryall of the tyde." The apparent lack of tides convinced him that Hudson Strait was not a passage to the west.

drifting icebergs pushed his ships back and hid any passage that might lead them through to the Orient.

Toward the end of the 1500's, Dutch seamen and merchants became the chief rivals of England in finding a land or sea route to the riches of Cathay. For them a northeastern passage was more desirable because along the way they could trade with the Russians. The most important person in these Dutch Arctic explorations was Willem Barents, who was the chief pilot on three successive voyages. On his third expedition, which left Amsterdam in 1596, Barents hoped to get to the Kara Strait by sailing around the northern tip of Novaya Zemlya. By following a very northerly route Barents piloted the ships of the expedition through unexplored seas, discovering West Spitzbergen, the largest island in a group now called Svalbard, before he turned eastward. But ice began to close in around his ship as it approached Novaya Zemlya, and gradually the ice pressed itself so hard around the ship that the hull was forced upward. When the ship finally burst out of the ice it was so cracked and damaged that the Dutchmen had to abandon it and seek shelter on the coast of Novaya Zemlya.

Thus began the first wintering of European explorers so far north and one we know about from the descriptions of one of the men who experienced it. From the timbers they had salvaged from their abandoned ship the Dutchmen built themselves a house, which they furnished with sleeping bunks, lamps, and all the remaining equipment they could haul from the frozen and disintegrating hull.

As the winter wore on the cold became so extreme that the wine froze and sheets became like stiff white boards. Then the supplies of bear fat began to run out. The smoke from the fire inside the house became so suffocating that the men had to stay in bed and keep warm as best they could from the hot stones that they put around their feet.

Somehow the Dutchmen managed to survive the winter but with little hope of ever being rescued. Willem Barents was convinced in fact that their only way of ever getting back to Amsterdam was to make a boat journey to the nearest mainland, which was the Kola Peninsula 1,600 miles away.

By mid-June the courageous men of his expedition managed to prepare themselves for another perilous experience. They loaded the ship's boats with all the cargo they could hold and set out. By using every means they knew—rowing, sailing, and even dragging the boats from one water channel to another—the Dutchmen completed the remarkable journey to the Kola Peninsula. But they arrived without Barents. A day or so after the start of the last stage of the expedition that he knew was so necessary, he had died.

With the return of Barents' expedition the Dutch interest in finding the Northeast Passage came to an end. It was left to the English to resume the search that they directed first to the east and then to the west. In 1610 Henry Hudson was commissioned by some English merchants to follow the inlets that John Davis had seen and to find for England a route through the northwest. As Hudson sailed through Hudson Strait and into the bay that was later named for him, he was convinced that this was the route to Cathay.

Six years later another English navigator and explorer, William Baffin came very near to solving the mystery of the Northwest Passage. He took his 50-ton ship the *Discovery* up the west coast of Greenland to Melville Bay before going westward. Then he sailed close by Jones Sound and into Lancaster Sound before being forced by the ice to turn back toward home. Both these sounds—although Baffin never knew this—lead into the open waters of the Beaufort Sea. From there to the Bering Sea would have been relatively easy going for the sturdy *Discovery*.

All during this period of Arctic exploration by the English and the Dutch, Russia was extending its power eastward across the enormous expanse of Siberia. By the late 1600's, Russian control stretched all the way to the Kamchatka Peninsula on the Pacific Ocean. Then, in 1725, Czar Peter the Great conceived the idea of a series of exploratory journeys by which he hoped the entire northern coast of Siberia would be discovered and mapped. To Vitus Bering,

Above: Peter the Great, who planned the Great Northern Expedition to map the northern Siberian coastline. He also commissioned the Dane Vitus Bering to discover if North America was joined to Asia, or if a passage separated them.

Above: a map drawn by order of Vitus Bering in 1729, illustrating his first expedition of 1727–1729. The map shows the people of Siberia as observed by Bering, and also records the line of soundings to above 67 degrees north. It was there that Bering decided "our task had been carried out and that the land did not extend farther north."

a Dane, he gave a formidable task. First of all Bering and 25 men would trek overland for more than 6,000 miles across Europe and Asia to Okhotsk on the Pacific Coast. From there they would make a sea voyage around the Kamchatka Peninsula and try to land on the American coast.

Despite the rigors of this vast expedition that involved the transportation of men and supplies over four of the largest rivers in Russia, Bering and his companions persevered. Once they managed to reach Okhotsk, they were then subjected to the frustration of waiting as ships for their voyage around Kamchatka Peninsula were made ready. Finally, in 1728, after nearly two years of waiting around, Bering was able to take ship with another Russian explorer named Alexei Chirikov from the east coast of the Kamchatka Peninsula. The expedition sailed northward as far as the Gulf of Anadyr. From there they passed an island that Bering named St. Lawrence and entered the Bering Strait. But because it was then

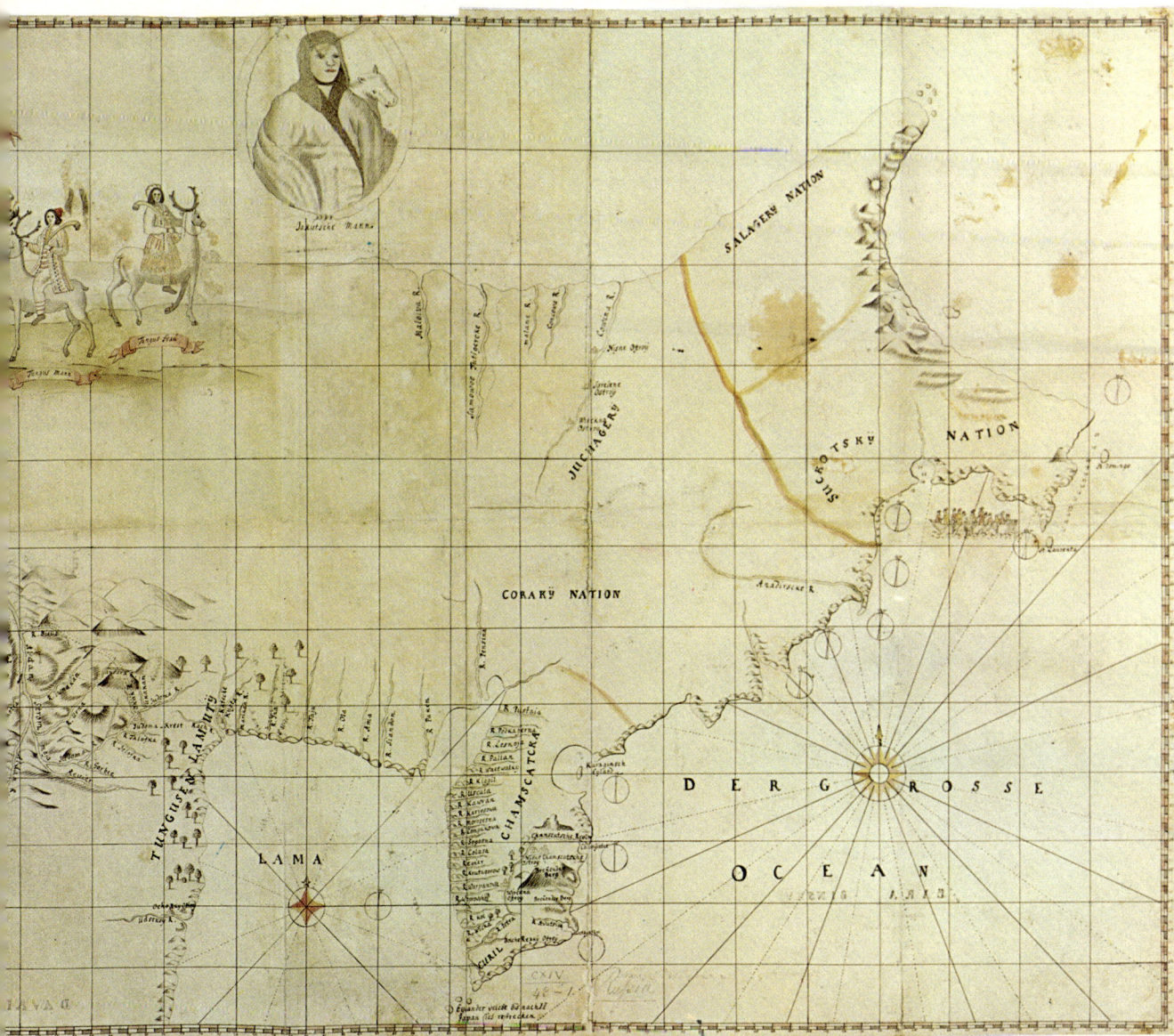

Below: a painted wooden figure of a European trader, probably a Russian, carved by an Indian on Vancouver Island. After Bering's landing in the Aleutian Islands, the Russians came trading as far south as San Francisco.

late summer and ice might at any moment close in, Bering decided to return to Okhotsk and then make his way back to St. Petersburg.

It was not until 1741 that he succeeded in completing the ambitious plans of exploration that Peter the Great had presented to him 16 years earlier. Aboard a ship called the *St. Peter* Bering, again accompanied by Chirikov, sailed northeastward from Okhotsk, sighting Mount Saint Elias in southeastern Alaska and landing on Kayak Island. Within a few years of Bering's landing on the American coast other Russians made contact with Alaskan Eskimos and were making trading voyages as far south as San Francisco.

During this same period, Englishmen were beginning to explore the Canadian interior and its coastline to the north. Yet it was not until the early 1800's that the golden age of Arctic exploration arrived. The British Navy took the lead in a general revival of interest in finding a Northwest Passage. What the British government hoped its navy would accomplish was the circumnavigation and exploration of the Arctic coast of Canada and the discovery of any new land to the north of North America.

This desire for more Arctic territories was in part due to Britain's fear of Russia's imperialistic interests in the Arctic. After Bering's landing on the Alaskan coast, Russian traders and hunters came to the region, and in 1784, established the first white settlement in Alaska on Kodiak Island. Then the Russians organized their own trading firm and this became the only governing power in Alaska.

So great was Britain's desire to counteract Russian operations in

Below: Sir John Ross, who commanded one of the naval squadrons that sailed north in 1818. He came to be called "Croker Mountain" Ross for the chain of mountains that he thought he saw just off Lancaster Sound, blocking his way to the west. He was mocked for lack of courage after his return. In 1829, Ross headed another expedition to find a Northwest Passage. It was during this voyage that his nephew, James Clark Ross located the North Magnetic Pole on Boothia Peninsula.

the Arctic that in 1818 Parliament offered a financial reward for the discovery of a Northwest Passage or for an attempt on the North Pole. By May of the same year a large Arctic expedition had been organized that involved two separate squadrons. One of these was to get as near to the North Pole as possible and the other was to sail up Davis Strait and search for an entrance to the Northwest Passage.

The man in charge of the latter squadron was Commander John Ross, and he had as his second-in-command a young officer who was to become an outstanding figure in Arctic exploration. This was Lieutenant Edward Parry. By the end of August, 1818, he and Ross had guided their two ships into Lanacaster Sound, which was considered to be the most likely route through to the northwest. The *Isabella* and the *Alexander* sailed westward through the sound for only a day when Ross suddenly gave the order to stop. Ahead of him he "distinctly saw land round the bottom of the bay forming a chain of mountains connected with those which extended along the north and south side." Parry and the other men on board could see nothing ahead but clear sea. So convinced was Ross that he saw mountains that he named them the Croker Mountains in honor of a secretary of the British Admiralty and gave the order for the *Isabella* and the *Alexander* to sail eastward to England.

When the expedition returned the story of Ross' Croker Mountains grew into a myth that many people considered had been nothing more than a convenient excuse for returning to safer waters. Gossip became so damaging to the navy's reputation that a second expedition was organized to settle the question of the Croker

Mountains in Lancaster Sound. This time Edward Parry was put in command. On May 11, the *Hecla* and the *Griper* left England.

This voyage, which was to last for over a year, was to be the greatest single forward stride made in the discovery of a Northwest Passage. Parry was to take the *Hecla* and the *Griper* into one of the most likely passages by which a seaway between the Atlantic and the Pacific could be established.

When the two ships reached Lancaster Sound, their crews listened for the reports from the men high up in the crow's-nests. Longitude 83° 12′ was reached with the shores of the sound miles apart and no Croker Mountains visible.

By the end of August, the *Hecla* and the *Griper* entered an even broader strait now known as Barrow Strait. They had a wide seaway to the west with room to maneuver between the large floes of ice. By early September, they had passed through Melville Sound and had crossed the meridian of 110° West from Greenwich England—a position in the Arctic Ocean that lies due north from the center of the state of Montana. All the men on board the *Hecla* and the *Griper* by having achieved this westward position became entitled to a reward of £5,000 (worth about $50,000 in today's money) under the Parliamentary Act of 1818. But there was little time for celebrations. Already Parry could see as he climbed to the crow's-nest of the *Hecla* an impenetrable barrier of ice stretching across their path. There was no sign of any open sea. The two ships anchored at a position slightly to the east of Cape Hearne. As they waited for the possibility that the ice might loosen up, the temperature continued to drop and the *Hecla* and the *Griper* were forced to put into a nearby bay to wait out the winter.

It was to be a long and dark one with 100 days of total darkness that began in the first week of November. However, in terms of good health and morale, it was to be a remarkable one. Parry made sure that the men had few idle moments for thoughts of home. A strict regime of work and exercise was established and in the evenings there was dancing and singing. Every two weeks a play was put on and every week the expedition's own newspaper—the *North Georgia Gazette and Winter Chronicle* was published.

In August 1821, Parry made one last attempt to take the *Hecla* and the *Griper* through the ice that had blocked their westward progress in the previous year. But the floes even in August were 50 feet thick and made impossible his plan to navigate the Northwest Passage. Parry was forced to return to England.

In 1824, however, Parry was back in the Arctic. This time he explored the waters to the south of Baffin Island and wintered over for two years. Still the ice defeated him.

The British for a while stopped thinking of reaching the Indies by way of a Northwest Passage. Instead, they started thinking of getting to the North Pole. Because he was the outstanding figure in Arctic exploration during this period, Edward Parry was the obvious man to make this first attempt on the pole.

Right: The Arctic Ocean, showing the routes of explorers who for almost 300 years tried to find a Northwest or a Northeast Passage to the Orient.

....	Willoughby & Chancellor	1	1553
	Willoughby	1A	1553–4
	Chancellor	1B	1553–4
— — —	Frobisher	2a	1576
		2b	1577
		2c	1578
....	Davis	3a	1585
		3b	1586
		3c	1587
————	Barents	4a	1594
	Barents	4A	1594
	Other members of expedition	4B	1594
	Barents (with Linschoten)	4b	1595
	Barents	4c	1596–7
	Expedition after death of Barents	4C	1597
— — —	Hudson	5a	1607
		5b	1608
		5c	1609
		5d	1610–1
————	Baffin (with Bylot)	6a	1615
		6b	1616
— — —	Bering	7a	1725–7
	Bering (with Chirikov)	7b	1728–9
	Bering (with Chirikov)	7c	1740–1
	Chirikov (after death of Bering)	7C	1741–2
....	Ross, John (with Parry & Ross, James C.)	8a	1818
	Buchan (with Franklin)	8b	1818
	Ross, John	8c	1829–33
————	Parry (with Ross, James C.)	9a	1819–20
		9b	1821–3
		9c	1824–5
		9d	1827

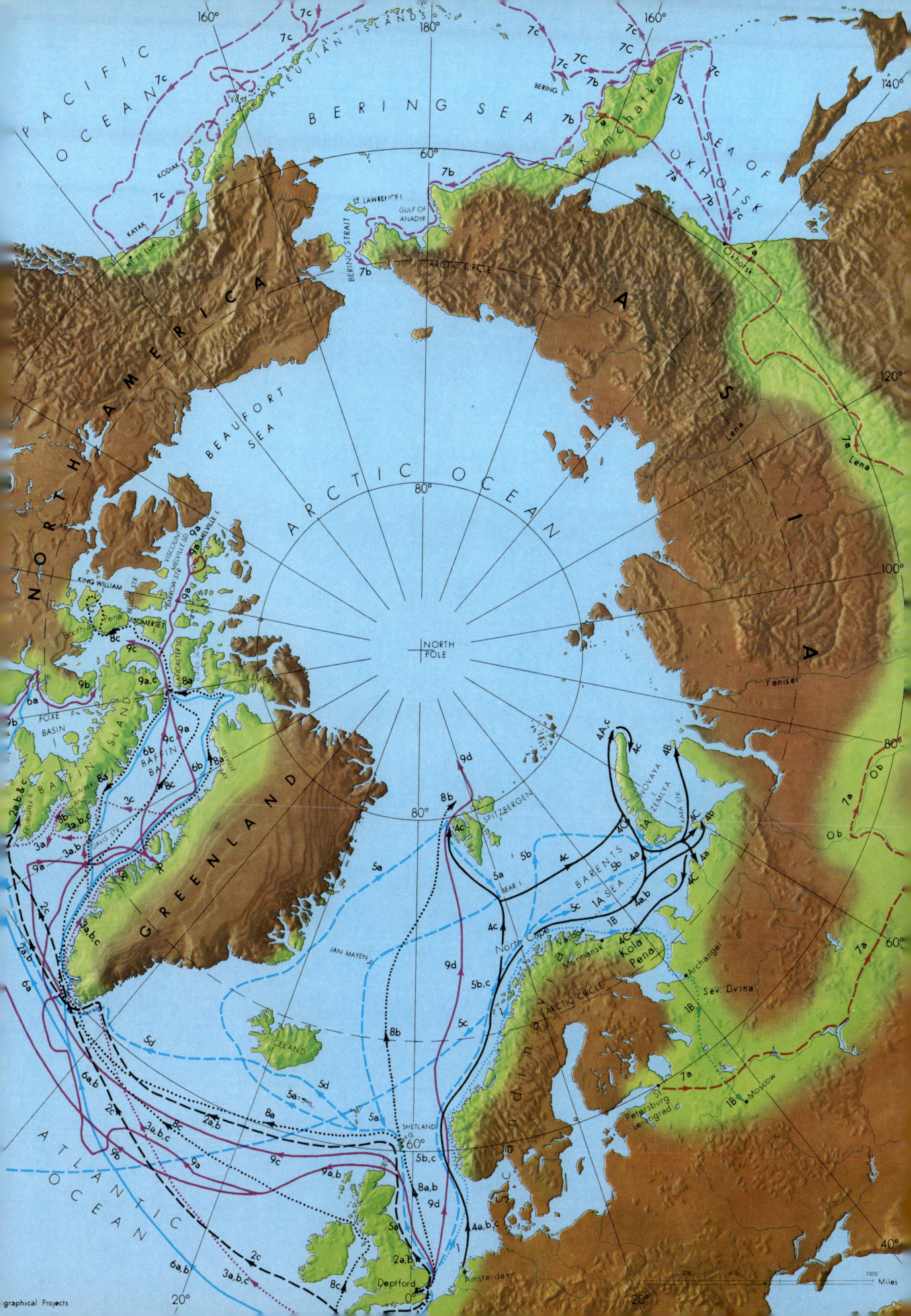

With an expedition of 28 men he sailed north to Spitzbergen in the late spring of 1827. From Trurenberg Bay in Spitzbergen he and his party proceeded over the ice. They took with them two boats shod along their keels with strips of iron. Whenever they had to cross ice the boats were dragged by the sturdiest men who accompanied Parry. When they came to open water the boats were launched and used as boats again.

In this way Parry and his men pushed on toward the pole until the end of July when they had reached latitude 82° 45′ N.—within

500 miles of the North Pole. At this point they were forced to turn back, but the record position they had achieved was to remain unbeaten for the next 48 years.

The year after this polar journey one more attempt was made to find a Northwest Passage. "Croker Mountain" Ross was in command of this expedition and he had with him as his second-in-command his nephew, James Clark Ross, a very talented commander who had made a number of previous Arctic journeys. Although the expedition ran into difficulties from the beginning because of the steam-powered engine used to propel the *Victory,* Ross managed to get the expedition to the east coast of Somerset Island. From here he turned south, sailing past Bellot Strait where he began to run into thick ice. As winter approached he was forced to make a landfall on the east coast of the Boothia Peninsula, where the *Victory* was to remain stuck for three winters. During the enforced stay James Clark Ross made good use of his time. He studied the dress and sledging techniques of the Eskimos who had a settlement near the *Victory,*

Above left: a watercolor by Sir John Ross showing two Eskimos, Ikmalik and Apelaglui, sketching the coast of King William Island while sitting on board the *Victory* when it was caught in the ice. This was painted during Ross' second voyage searching for the Northwest Passage, from 1829 to 1833.

and with them he made long sledging journeys across the ice to King William Island. The younger Ross was also very interested in the study of magnetism and was eager to find the North Magnetic Pole. This he knew to be a mysterious spot in the Northern Hemisphere toward which the north-seeking compass needle points. The spot at that time lay somewhere in the region where the *Victory* was stuck. On May 31, 1831, James Clark Ross located the exact position of the North Magnetic Pole on Boothia Peninsula.

Eventually, after three winters had passed, the men on board the *Victory* were forced to abandon it and make their way by the ship's boats to Lancaster Sound. Here they were lucky enough to be picked up by a whaling ship and returned with it to England.

A Northwest Passage to Cathay had yet to be discovered. The dream of explorers for four centuries was to remain undiscovered until the summer of 1906. Nevertheless the idea of successfully traversing the northern route between the Atlantic and the Pacific was to continue to attract explorers during the intervening years.

Above: James Clark Ross on the ice, shooting musk ox, in a watercolor by his uncle, Sir John Ross, during their stay on the *Victory* in the Arctic. Both uncle and nephew spent a lot of time with the Eskimos. James Clark Ross used their sledging techniques to reach the North Magnetic Pole.

Above: a Wedgwood portrait medallion of Captain James Cook, one of many such medallions of contemporary famous people made by the firm of Josiah Wedgwood. Cook's superb navigational abilities—as well as his gifts of leadership—were appreciated by the authorities, and he was the obvious choice to make the voyage in search of the Southern Continent.

The Great Southland

3

Even as late as the 1770's the idea of an unknown southern land—Terra Australis Incognita—still persisted. Somewhere below the bottom of Africa and the terrifying waters of Cape Horn there was a rich land, and the British government wanted to be the first to find it. In 1772 they commissioned Captain James Cook to begin the second of his famous voyages into the South Pacific—this time to solve the riddle of the great Southern Continent. He was given two ships, the *Resolution* and the *Adventure*, and in mid-July, 1772, they sailed from Plymouth, England. Because the two ships kept getting separated during the three-year voyage, most of what we know about the expedition concerns the *Resolution*, which Cook commanded.

After passing south through the Atlantic and turning east around the Cape of Good Hope, Cook kept the ships as far south as the drifting ice permitted. On January 17, 1773, both of them crossed the Antarctic Circle, an imaginary circle of the earth parallel to the equator and forming the border of Antarctica. The men in Cook's expedition became the first to cross into the southern polar region— one of only a few genuine "firsts" in modern exploration. For after all, Stone Age men had preceded the explorers who first landed on places such as Iceland, Greenland, North America, Australia, and Easter Island.

The *Adventure* and the *Resolution* continued sailing south from the Antarctic Circle for a few hours but the seemingly endless

Above: Cook's ships, the *Resolution* and the *Adventure,* collecting water by taking on ice at 61 degrees south. The watercolor is by W. Hodges, who was on Cook's voyages of 1773.

37

Above: a watercolor of a penguin by George Forster, a naturalist who accompanied Captain Cook on the 1773 journey when they were the first to cross the Antarctic Circle, although they did not sight Antarctica.

pack ice that stretched out before them forced Cook to turn northward and then to the east.

During the Antarctic "summers" of the two succeeding years the *Resolution* crossed the Antarctic Circle again and unknowingly got to within only 150 miles of the Antarctic shore. By the spring of 1775, when he rounded Cape Horn and headed for England, James Cook had sailed completely around the continent without sighting land. In his journal Cook made a forbidding prediction about Antarctica: "The risk one runs in exploring a coast in these unknown and icy seas is so very great that I can be bold enough to say that no man will ever venture farther than I have done, and that the lands which may lie to the south will never be explored."

James Cook's gloomy conclusions about Antarctic exploration were soon ignored by American and British seal and whale hunters. During the years between 1800 and 1820, they sighted many islands and parts of the Antarctic Peninsula as they pushed into Antarctic waters, testing tides and currents and ice conditions, always com-

peting with each other to find new regions to fish and fresh breeding places for seals.

One of these men, Nathaniel B. Palmer of Stonington, Connecticut, discovered what is now called Deception Island (one of the South Shetland Islands) as he looked for new seal-hunting grounds. Then one day from the slopes of a mountain on Deception he saw another island (Trinity Island) and possibly also the Antarctic Peninsula. After he reported what he had seen, Palmer was commissioned by the captain of his seal-hunting fleet to explore in the direction of the distant island. Palmer, who may have been the first man to sight the mainland of Antarctica, found in his explorations "an extensive mountain country, more sterile and dismal if possible, and more heavily laden with ice and snow than the South Shetlands. There were sea-leopards on its shore but no fur seals. The main part of its coast was ice bound, although it was midsummer in this hemisphere, and a landing consequently difficult."

While on his way back to the South Shetland Islands to meet up again with the American sealing fleet, Palmer's ship, the *Hero,* became enveloped in a thick fog. Rather than risk a collision with an iceberg Palmer decided to anchor for the night. When he came on deck to stand watch and struck the ship's bell to toll the time, he heard through the fog the sound of an echoing bell. Half an hour later, the same thing happened again—Palmer struck two bells and heard the reply of two bells. Each half hour for the rest of the night came the ghostly echo.

Finally, in the morning, when the fog lifted, the men on board the *Hero* were amazed to see that their tiny sloop lay between two other sloops. When the American flag was hoisted, the other ships each hoisted an Imperial Russian flag.

Then a Russian sloop sent its boat to the *Hero* and invited Palmer aboard. He learned that the ships had been sent by the Russian czar to make a round-the-world voyage under the command of Captain Fabian von Bellingshausen. It is not clear from the records just how Palmer and Bellingshausen managed to converse, but presumably the Russians had an English-speaking person with them, or perhaps a few of the Russians could speak some English. On their way from Kronshtadt, on the Gulf of Finland, to the Antarctic Circle they had spent a month in England while they waited for charts and navigating instruments that were being prepared for them in London. They must have understood some English because during their stay they went sightseeing in London and even went to the theater.

The Russian expedition had sailed almost entirely around Antarctica, always within sight of the ice pack. Late in January, 1821, before his meeting with Palmer, Bellingshausen had discovered a small island in the Bellinghausen Sea and named it Peter I Island. At the end of January the *Vostok* and the *Mirnyi* sailing eastward had sighted land again and named it Alexander I Land after the czar. "I call this discovery 'land'," he wrote to the czar, "because its

Above: U.S. sealer Nathaniel B. Palmer, discoverer of Deception Island.
Below: James Weddell, who went 214 nautical miles farther south than Cook, searching for new sealing grounds. He found what is now called the Weddell Sea. Although his ship was fitted only for sealing, Weddell did what he could to make careful scientific observations, taking readings of the temperature of the water and observing the currents.

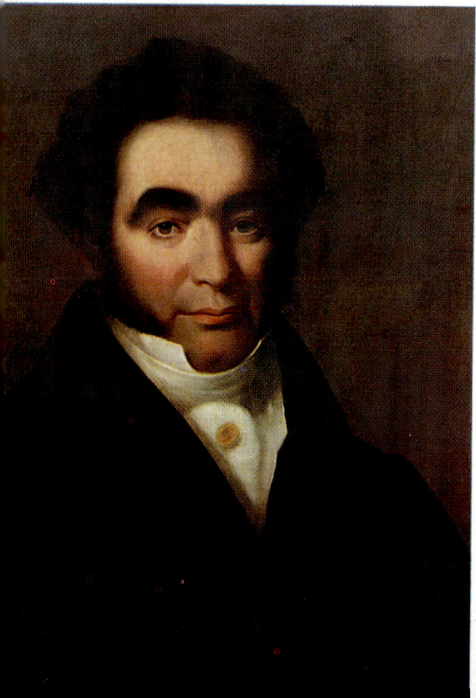

southern extent disappeared beyond the range of our vision." Later explorers were to find that what Bellingshausen had seen was really a large island separated from the mainland of Antarctica by a narrow strait 200 miles long.

During the next 15 years, the waters around the newly discovered continent were the scene of continued activity by the sealers. Another American seal-hunter, Captain John Davis of New Haven, may have been the first to actually set foot on Antarctica on February 7, 1821. After leaving Deception Island he found land to the south. Davis anchored his ship in Hughes Bay. The land, Davis noted in his log, was "high and covered entirely with snow." A party went ashore but found no seals. When he left, Davis wrote, "I think this Southern Land to be a Continent."

In the same year a British sealer named James Weddell sailed his two ships, the brig *Jane* and the smaller ship *Beaufoy*, to the South Orkney Islands and then turned south to look for new sealing lands. The two ships made their way through one of the most dangerous of Antarctic seas—made so by the great pressure of the circulating ice within it—until they reached the latitude 74° 15′ S.

Because the seal-hunting season was almost over and winter was just about to set in, Weddell decided to turn northward again. In order to cheer up his crew, who were disappointed that they had found no seals that in turn would pay their wages, Weddell made

Left: Palmer's little sloop between two big Russian sloops of war. Caught in the fog, Palmer had anchored, and when the fog lifted was astonished to find himself in between the two ships of Captain Bellingshausen.

Below: the Russian Captain Fabian von Bellingshausen, who commanded an Antarctic expedition to 70° S. latitude.

a little ceremony. The Union Jack was hoisted aboard both ships and the cannon were fired in honor of the men who had accompanied Weddell to the farthest south point so far attained—214 nautical miles nearer to the South Pole than Captain Cook had reached.

In the years between 1830 and 1850 exploration in both the Arctic and Antarctic became involved with the phenomenon of the earth's magnetism. This was the beginning of the era of larger and faster steamships that needed to be navigated by more precise compasses, which in turn involved a better understanding of magnetism. For centuries sailors and explorers had been aware of the north and south magnetic poles. A piece of magnetite hanging from a string would turn until it was pointing north and south, thus enabling sailors to tell in which direction they were sailing, even in a storm when they could not see the stars.

The earth has north and south magnetic poles in addition to its north and south geographic poles. But the magnetic and geographic poles are not located at the same places. The North Magnetic Pole that James Clark Ross located in 1831 was on the Boothia Peninsula in northern Canada, and about 1,000 miles from the North Geographic Pole.

It was predicted in the 1830's that the South Magnetic Pole would be discovered in the region of latitude 66°S. and longitude 146°E. Within a few years three expeditions were organized to find its

exact location. Britain put James Clark Ross in charge of theirs, King Louis Philippe of France commissioned Dumont d'Urville to go to Antarctica for "the glory of France." The youthful United States made its first venture into large-scale exploration by dispatching Lieutenant Charles Wilkes and a squadron of ships to investigate the Antarctic.

D'Urville of France was the first to get away. He had been planning an expedition to the South Pacific, but when the king heard about Britain's plans he sent word to d'Urville saying that he must explore the Antarctic region. Because d'Urville was mainly inter-

Above: the French ships, the *Astrolabe* and the *Zelee*, in the dreaded storm belt between the latitudes of 50 and 60 degrees south. When the visibility was poor because of fog or snowstorms, the ships maintained contact by firing a gun every half hour or ringing bells.
Left: Jules Dumont d'Urville, the commander of the French expedition in search of the South Magnetic Pole. A naval officer, he was a linguist, explorer, and ethnologist as well, who in the course of a varied career had rescued the Venus de Milo for posterity.

ested in studying the people who live on the Pacific Islands, he was not enthusiastic about the royal command.

Nevertheless, with two ships, the *Astrolabe* and the *Zelee*, the Frenchman set out in September, 1837. Since d'Urville's original plan had been to explore the tropics the vessels were not properly designed or outfitted for a voyage to Antarctica. As the *Astrolabe* and the *Zelee* pushed on through the southern ocean, their wide gunports admitted cascades of icy water into the holds. By January, 1838, however, they had reached the Weddell Sea and were making their way southward in an attempt to beat Weddell's record.

43

They got only as far as 63° 39′ S. when the pack ice closed in around them. For two frustrating months d'Urville's ships skirted the ice in an attempt to find a clear route, but they managed only to hover along the edge of the ice. Finally, they turned northward to spend the rest of the Antarctic summer of 1838 exploring the Graham Land tip of the Palmer Peninsula. Then for the remaining months of that year and for most of the following one d'Urville cruised the South Pacific.

On January 1, 1840, he turned his ships toward the Antarctic again, this time sailing south from Hobart, Tasmania. On January 19, Dumont d'Urville sighted land—a panorama of ice and snow fronted by towering ice cliffs that stretched far to the east and west, broken occasionally by deep recesses where the icebergs that littered the sea had fallen away. This he named Adelie Land after

Above: an engraving after a sketch by the expedition artist Louis Le Breton (who was also the ship's surgeon). It shows part of d'Urville's crew landing on the frozen shores of Adelie Land.

Right: the crewmen of the *Astrolabe* celebrating the discovery of Adelie Land. Dumont d'Urville wrote that the men "summoned *Father Antarctic* on deck. They presented all kinds of quaint scenes; there was a masked procession, a sermon, and a banquet. It all ended with dancing and a song."

his wife and dispatched a boat to explore France's Antarctic possession. Once they had got to the cliff, however, the Frenchmen found it too steep and icy for a landing. But they did manage to unfurl the French flag on a small rocky islet very near Adelie Land—to a chorus of squawks from a group of penguins—called Adélie penguins by d'Urville.

The South Magnetic Pole lay farther to the east and the spinning compass needle indicated that it could not be far away. While the *Astrolabe* and the *Zelee* were heading in the direction of the pole, they were involved in another of those chance encounters that seem to defy all odds. By 1841, the British and American expeditions to the South Magnetic Pole had got underway. Yet what were the chances of two of these expeditions meeting along the 13,800-mile coastline of the Antarctic? On January 29, the *Astrolabe* and the *Zelee* were wallowing through a heavy fog. Suddenly, the lookout spotted a man-of-war flying the Stars and Stripes bearing down upon them. It was the *Porpoise,* one of Lieutenant Wilkes' fleet that had been commissioned by the United States Navy.

Above: the *Astrolabe* leaving the icy polar sea. By this time the ship had been away from home for almost three years. Although d'Urville had been unable to go farther than Weddell, he had claimed Adelie Land for France.

D'Urville immediately ordered the sails raised so that he could meet the Americans. But the captain of the *Porpoise* misunderstood this maneuver. He thought that the French ships were trying to keep their exploration a secret by sailing away, so he gave orders for the *Porpoise* to make its way through the fog.

Shortly after this encounter d'Urville reached another icy coast that seemed to extend indefinitely and prevent further movement south. The men aboard the *Astrolabe* and *Zelee* had been away from home for almost three years, and must have welcomed the order to turn the ships away from the icy cliffs and head for France. Even though more than a century was to pass before another French expedition entered Antarctica, d'Urville's discoveries there did result in France's claim to the thin wedge of territory that extends from the coast of Adelie Land to the South Pole.

When Dumont d'Urville returned to France he claimed that he had first sighted the Antarctic on January 18. Lieutenant Wilkes was later to make the statement that he had been the first to find land in the same region of Antarctica—on January 19. Wilkes, it turned out, had been first after all. For d'Urville had crossed the International Date Line in his voyage but had failed to advance the date in his log. So land had been seen on the 19th by both explorers, but Wilkes had seen it first. According to his log, the young American lieutenant had sighted the continent some 10 hours before Dumont d'Urville.

The United States expedition commanded by Charles Wilkes had

sailed from Hampton Roads, Virginia in August, 1838. It was the most ill-prepared and probably the unhappiest expedition that ever sailed to Antarctica. The ships selected were unsuitable and Wilkes proved to be an impetuous and over strict commander.

None of the ships was fortified against the ice and heavy weather and the large square gunports were left wide open for the surge of icy southern seas. There were three warships in the expedition—the *Vincennes,* the *Peacock,* and the *Porpoise*—together with two smaller ships, which served as tenders to the larger ones, and a supply ship, which proved to be so slow that it was sent home early in the expedition.

Six months after leaving Virginia the expedition assembled itself for the first push into the Antarctic at Orange Harbor, Nassau Bay in the south of Tierra del Fuego. The *Porpoise,* with Wilkes aboard, and one of the tenders made for the Weddell Sea, which proved to be much icier than it had been at the time of Weddell's voyage. At the same time the *Peacock* and another of the tenders, the *Flying Fish,* went westward in hopes of getting as far as Captain Cook's 105°W. By riding above the ice and slipping through narrow leads the *Flying Fish* only just failed to reach 71° 10'S., which had been Cook's most southerly point.

Then in May, 1839, when winter had come to the Antarctic, the United States expedition made its way into the warmer waters of the Pacific Ocean. It was to be seven months before the ships were able to go south again. When they again entered the Antarctic

Above: Sir James Clark Ross. He was experienced in arctic conditions, and had two ideal ships to cope with the ice. It was his ambition to match his discovery of the North Magnetic Pole by claiming the southern one as well.

region early in 1840, the men on board got their first glimpse of land when they sighted one of the Balleny Islands, which of course had already been claimed by the British sealer John Balleny.

The *Peacock* and the *Vincennes* then went westward, following the coast of a belt of packed ice. Along the way the *Peacock* was wrecked and broken up by a collision with an iceberg, so the westward push that Wilkes was so keen to accomplish was made by the *Vincennes* and the *Porpoise*. He was convinced that if he could penetrate the ice belt that lay to the south he would reach land. At the end of January he saw his chance to take the ships safely between the massive islands of ice into a bay. This bay, which he calculated to be 140° 30′ E. and in latitude 66° 45′ S., was backed up by land rising to the south, and stretching east and west for 60 miles (probably in the vicinity of Adelie Land). Here Wilkes confidently announced the existence of the Antarctic continent, and called the bay they had sailed into Piner's Bay, after one of his crewmen. It was during this period that the *Porpoise,* sailing independently of the *Vincennes,* met Dumont d'Urville's ships.

For most of the time they cruised along the Antarctic continent the men on board the *Vincennes* were in great discomfort. Every rope and every inch of deck was thickly encrusted with ice and the hold of the ship was too small to accommodate the men properly. Moreover, the clothing issued to them was absurdly inadequate for polar weather. It is not surprising that the crewmen shown in the illustrations of the journey look white and chilled and scantily dressed for the occasion.

By mid-February, 1840, the *Vincennes* encountered a vast peninsula of ice that jutted out into the sea and blocked any further progress. Wilkes had nevertheless managed to get west of Sabrina Land to longitude 97° 37′ E., even though he had now to give up his idea of getting as far west as Enderby Land. The *Vincennes* turned northeast again with the *Porpoise* trailing it. In his journal Wilkes remarked, "I have seldom seen so many happy faces or such rejoicing as the announcement of my intention to return produced." By mid-March, Wilkes was in Sydney Harbour, Australia, having completed a remarkable voyage despite the frailty of the ships and the poor food and the flimsy clothing that had been supplied for the expedition. Wilkes and his men had traveled along 1,500 miles of Antarctic coast, by far the most important cruise to the south polar region yet undertaken.

Even though the idea of searching for the South Magnetic Pole had begun in England, it was not until 1839 that the government voted the necessary funds. James Clark Ross was put in charge of the expedition and given two ships from the Royal Navy, the *Erebus* and the *Terror*. Both were small, slow, and clumsy and, unlike Wilkes' ships, they were perfect for making their way through the ice. They had sturdy hulls, watertight bulkheads to prevent flooding in case of a collision with an iceberg, and decks of double thickness. Warm clothes were issued to the men. Canned meats and

Right: the *Terror* taking on water during the expedition led by James Clark Ross, in a watercolor by I. E. Davis. The men are cutting into the icecap, which will then be melted.

Right: taking possession of Possession Island in 1841. A landing had to be made to make a proper claim to the land for the British sovereign, but the coast of the mainland was inaccessible because of ice. They therefore made the landing on a little rocky islet.

vegetables, which were relative innovations at that time, were put in the holds. The staple diet of the sailors on such a voyage was dried meat and dried biscuits, so the addition of properly preserved canned food would provide a welcome variety for the long voyage to the Antarctic.

In September, 1839, the *Erebus* and the *Terror* sailed from the River Thames out into the English Channel and began the first leg of their journey to Australia. This was to take the expedition 11 months to accomplish, and the ships docked at Hobart, Tasmania, in August, 1840.

While they were being refitted and made ready for the Antarctic, Ross received word from London that both d'Urville and Wilkes had been cruising in the region where he was planning to search for the South Magnetic Pole. Angry at the "embarrassing situation" that the two explorers had placed him in, he decided to explore the coast to the east of where the others had investigated.

On November 12, 1840, the *Erebus* and the *Terror* left for Antarctica and in less than two months they were in the great belt of floating icebergs that had almost destroyed Wilkes' ships. The two sturdy ships slowly battered their way through the pack until January 9, when they finally broke out of the crushing pack ice. Ahead of them lay open sea with no land in sight. They were free to continue sailing on toward Antarctica. Ross ordered a course of due south, confident that the South Magnetic Pole was within reach.

Then land was sighted far ahead of the ships. Towering peaks rose for thousands of feet above the sea. The men on board the *Erebus* and the *Terror* saw mountains, "perfectly covered with eternal snow, which rose to elevations varying from seven- to ten-thousand feet above the level of the ocean. The glaciers that filled their intervening valleys, and which descended from the mountains' summits, projected in many places several miles into the sea."

By January 12, Ross was only a few miles off the mainland that he called Victoria Land in honor of Queen Victoria. He and his second-in-command, Francis Crozier, landed on a small island and named it Possession Island. Then continuing on, the *Erebus* and the

Above: the Ross Ice Shelf. The shelf is in constant movement, going toward the sea at a rate of about five feet a day. There the tides make large pieces break off at the edge, especially at the end of the Antarctic summer.

Right: Antarctica, showing the routes of the explorers who, in the years between 1772 and 1843, succeeded in establishing the approximate size and position of Antarctica.

SOUTH ATLANTIC OCEAN

SOUTH GEORGIA

FALKLAND IS.

TIERRA DEL FUEGO

PACIFIC OCEAN

SOUTH ORKNEYS

SOUTH SHETLAND IS.

DECEPTION I.

Graham Land Palmer Pena.

ALEXANDER I.

PETER I. I.

BELLINGSHAUSEN SEA

WEDDELL SEA

ANTARCTICA

SOUTH POLE

Ross Ice Shelf

ROSS SEA

ROSS I. MT. EREBUS
MT. TERROR McMURDO SOUND

Victoria Land

POSSESSION IS.

Sabrina Land

Adelie Land

BALLENY IS.

AUCKLAND IS.

ANTARCTIC CIRCLE

INDIAN OCEAN

Cape Town

C. Horn

VAN DIEMEN'S LAND
TASMANIA

Hobart

AUSTRALIA

NEW ZEALAND

INDIAN OCEAN

Cook	1a	1772-3	
(parts of his second voyage)	1b	1774	
	1c	1774-5	
Bellingshausen	2	1819-21	
Weddell	3	1822-3	
D'Urville	4	1837-40	
Wilkes	5	1838-40	
Ross, James C. (with Crozier)	6a	1839-41	
Ross, James C. (with Crozier)	6b	1841-2	
Ross, James C. (with Crozier)	6c	1842-3	

0 200 400 600 800 1000 Miles

© Geographical Projects

Terror reached the southerly position of 74° 20', thus beating the record Weddell had set a quarter of the way around on the other side of the continent. Open water still stretched ahead of them.

Early on the morning of January 28, another island capped with mountains was sighted. Coming closer, the men on board the two ships stared in disbelief at what they saw in this frigid land of ice and snow. Before them was an active volcano that gave off a stream of black smoke and spurts of flame. Ross named the steaming volcano Mount Erebus. An inactive volcano nearby was named Mount Terror.

Ross sailed along the northern edge of the island, still hoping to find a path toward the elusive South Magnetic Pole. Instead he came upon a sight even more spectacular than the volcano. Eastward from the island Ross saw a low, white line that stretched as far as the eye could see. "It presented an extraordinary appearance, gradually increasing in height as we got nearer to it, and proving to be a perpendicular cliff of ice between 150 and 200 feet above the level of the sea, perfectly flat and level at the top and without any fissures or promontories on its seaward face." Ross had discovered what is now called the Ross Ice Shelf—a vast slab of floating ice 600 to 1,000 feet thick that forms an almost impenetrable barrier to the interior of Antarctica.

From what he could see, Ross concluded that there could be no further progress toward the south and wrote in his log book, "We might with equal chance of success try to sail through the cliffs of Dover." So he decided to sail eastward, hoping to find a channel somewhere along the ice cliff. But by February 5, ice made further movement impossible, and the ships had to turn back toward Victoria Land. At McMurdo Sound, named for one of his officers, Ross gave up completely the idea of finding a way to the South Magnetic Pole. The *Erebus* and the *Terror* turned northward toward Tasmania.

In November, 1841, the British expedition explored almost the entire length of the ice shelf, and by the end of February, 1842, had reached 78° 10' south latitude, a record that was to stand for the next 60 years. But again the onset of another Antarctic winter forced them to withdraw before they had definitely established its eastern limits.

In November, 1842, Ross received permission from the British government to spend a third and final year in the Antarctic. His ambition this time was to combine a survey of the east coast of Graham Land with an attempt to achieve a record southerly position in the Weddell Sea. But he had not reckoned with the unaccountable changes in Antarctic weather or the position of the ice. The weather that season was one of constant gales, fogs, and snowstorms. At night the men had to keep themselves half awake, listening for the lookout's cry of "berg ahead" followed by the command "all hands on deck." Commander Crozier of the *Terror* never spent a night in his bed throughout that winter, preferring to take short naps in a

Above: the *Erebus* and the *Terror* caught in a storm. For Ross' expedition the weather could not have been worse. The two ships were in almost constant gales and storms. It was fortunate that they were almost perfectly suited for exploration in the polar waters.

chair or to be out on deck. James Weddell in his unprotected
sealer had reached 74° 15′ S. in 1823. A little south of 70° was all
that could be achieved by the sturdy *Erebus* and *Terror*, which had in
the previous year thrust their way through to the Ross Ice Shelf.
When his ships were stopped by the ice Ross gave up his ambitions
in the Weddell Sea and returned to England.

    After a lapse of about 50 years the British resumed their explora-
tions in Antarctica and it was the Ross Sea sector that was chosen as
starting point for British inland explorations of the continent.
Because this region provided the most accessible and the shortest
route to the heart of the continent, Britain's tragic race for the South
Pole was to begin in the Ross Sea.

Above: the Cross of the Guelphic Order of Hanover, Franklin's medal that was found in 1848 in the hands of the Eskimos—the first real evidence of the fate of the expedition that had set out to find the Northwest Passage.

LIEUT. FAIRHOLME.

CAPT. CROZIER.

JAMES REID (ICEMASTER)

S STANLEY (SURGEON)

The Search for Sir John Franklin

4

On May 19, 1845, the British explorer Sir John Franklin sailed from England with an expedition to search for the legendary Northwest Passage. His ships were the *Erebus* and the *Terror,* which had proved to be so seaworthy on James Clark Ross' expedition to the South Magnetic Pole. They were well stocked with provisions for a three-year journey to the icy wastes of the Arctic and back again. By the summer of 1847 nothing had been heard about the progress of Franklin and his men. Although everyone knew that there were still enough provisions on board, there was already a feeling of anxiety about the complete silence from the *Erebus* and the *Terror.*

The Hudson's Bay Company sent word to the Eskimos who roamed the Arctic to be on the lookout for the men from the expedition. The British government went so far as to offer a reward of £20,000 (worth about $300,000 in today's money) to any man of any nationality who rescued the missing men in Franklin's party.

The chill winter of 1847–1848 descended on Britain and with it still no news of Franklin—not a clue, not a word. Now the anxiety that had stimulated discussions in pubs and at garden parties the summer

CAPT. SIR JOHN FRANKLIN.

COMD'R FITZJAMES.

LIEUT. GRAHAM GORE.

H.D.S. GOODSIR (ASST. SURGEON)

C. OSMER (PURSER)

H.F. COLLINS (ICEMASTER)

before grew into a wave of concern. Inactivity fed the growing fear that all was not well with Franklin and his crew. Something had to be done and soon.

What route had Franklin taken? How might ice, wind, and storms have affected his course? Such questions had to be answered before a rescue mission could be organized and dispatched to the network of straits, bays, channels, and gulfs that made a forbidding maze of the yet-to-be-discovered Northwest Passage. But for every possible route suggested an alternative was proposed. Finally, the British government decided to send a massive rescue expedition.

Two ships would probe the Northwest Passage from the Bering Strait, while an overland expedition would trek northward from Canada. At the same time James Clark Ross would lead a third group that would approach the area from the east by sea. The Bering Strait expedition occupied themselves in exploring the waters north and west of the strait. The overland group, however, was forced to give up the Franklin search because of ice and storms.

James Clark Ross and his expedition got to the northeast end of

Above: some of the officers of the *Erebus,* which sailed from England on May 19, 1845, and was never heard from again. Franklin is in the middle of the upper row, wearing the medal shown opposite.

Above: the Arctic Council, the group set up to determine the fate of the Franklin expedition, planning the search in a painting by S. Pearce. James Clark Ross is the fourth from the left. On the wall behind them are portraits of Franklin and Sir John Barrow, who backed the expedition. Below: Lady Franklin, who became a popular heroine for her determination to continue the search for her husband.

Somerset Island where they spent the winter of 1848–1849. Traveling by foot and man-hauling their sledges they trekked 200 miles over Somerset Island hunting for signs of Franklin and his men. But it was to no avail and in 1849, when Ross returned to England, no more had been learned about the fate of the *Erebus* and the *Terror*.

Four years had now passed since Franklin had said goodbye to his wife Jane, and though almost all who searched for clues to the mysterious disappearance of Franklin and his men would eventually give up the quest, she continued to feel that somehow someone would eventually find her husband.

The following year more men and ships joined in the search for Franklin. Fifteen vessels and hundreds of men fanned out across ice, land, and water. The complicated maneuvers of the various search expeditions added to the details of Arctic geography and to the development of techniques of polar exploration. But they made no real advances in the evolution of polar exploration.

One of the search parties under the command of Captain Horatio Austin threaded its way through ice flows in Barrow Strait. Austin's small fleet, consisting of nine ships, came upon a barren, rocky bit of land called Beechey Island. Landing parties were sent ashore, although it was hard to believe that anyone would have chosen this forbidding place to camp. One of the parties was led by an American, Lieutenant E. J. De Haven, who commanded two small United States Navy brigs that had joined Austin's squadron. As De Haven scanned the bleak landscape, he saw an unusual object among the unpatterned rubble of rock and earth that formed the island. When he got nearer this obviously man-made feature, he saw that it consisted of a forge, the remains of a shooting gallery, and a storehouse. In the storehouse there were hundreds of cans of meat, stacked neatly in rows, coils of rope were piled up, empty bottles were scattered about. Was this all that remained of the Franklin expedition? Nearby, De Haven and his party found three tombstones. On one was roughly carved the name of John Torrinton, who had been the leading stoker of the *Terror*. The other two stones bore the names of two men from the *Erebus*. But what had become of the other missing men?

In 1853, Dr. John Rae, a Hudson's Bay Company official, set out on foot from northern Canada in search of the answer to this question. Slowly working his way northward, Rae and his companions reached Pelly Bay early in April, 1854. Pelly Bay leads out into the Gulf of Boothia, a body of frigid water that separates Baffin Island on the east from the Boothia Peninsula. From this Arctic area, Eskimos take their sledges over the ice to hunt for food.

When Dr. Rae encountered some of these Eskimos, he talked with them and learned that they had heard, from some other Eskimos, about a group of 40 white men seen several years before as they trudged south about 150 miles west of where Dr. Rae was. The strangers were hauling sledges and a small boat and talked about the

Below: among the many ships searching for Franklin was H.M.S. *Investigator,* here caught in the ice. The captain, Robert McLure, continued eastward by sledge after his ship was frozen into Prince of Wales Strait in 1850. He reached Melville Sound, which earlier explorers had reached coming from the east, and thus discovered the first of what later turned out to be several northwest passages to the Pacific Ocean.

two large ships they had had to abandon. They were heading for the Back River (also known as Back's "Fish River," or "Great Fish" River), but before they had got very far many of the men dropped in their tracks, apparently victims of exhaustion, scurvy, and hunger. Had any Eskimos seen the abandoned ships? Yes—not only seen but boarded. Where? Off the northwest coast of King William Island.

Any doubt of the truth of the Eskimos' report was quickly laid to rest when they produced cutlery, pieces of clothing, and other objects easily identified as having come from the *Erebus* and *Terror*. Dr. Rae concluded that there was little more to be learned at Pelly Bay and he set out toward the northwest. Along the way he met more Eskimos who gave him bits of information about the missing expedition. One story was particularly disturbing. According to Rae the Eskimos told of discovering "the corpses of some thirty persons and some graves . . . on the continent, and five dead bodies on an island near it, about a long day's journey to the northwest of the mouth of a large stream, which can be no other than Back's Fish River. . . . Some of the bodies were in a tent or tents, others were under the boat, which had been turned over to form a shelter, and some lay scattered about in different directions. . . . From the mutilated state of many of the bodies, and the contents of the kettles, it is evident that our wretched countrymen had been driven to the last dread alternative as a means of sustaining life [cannibalism]. . . ."

When Dr. Rae's report reached England, the news, though tragic, at least answered some of the questions that had been puzzling people for more than seven years. The British government was satisfied—although Dr. Rae pointed out that "None of the Esqi-

maux (Eskimos) with whom I had communication saw the "white men" either while living or after death, nor had they ever been at the place where the corpses were found, but had their information from natives who had been there. . . ." Nevertheless, the Franklin expedition was considered lost, and Dr. Rae was awarded £10,000 (about $150,000 in today's money) by the British government. It is not clear why the original reward of £20,000 was halved—perhaps because Rae had merely found evidence of the death of some of Franklin's men but had not managed to rescue any of them.

For Lady Franklin and for many people there still remained the question of what had become of Franklin himself? What had been the fate of the 100 men still unaccounted for? The British Government decided, however, that further expensive expeditions would not solve the mystery, and Lady Franklin's request for a resumed search was turned down.

She then arranged for a privately sponsored mission and purchased and outfitted a small steamer called the *Fox*. Leopold McClintock, who had been on an earlier search, was put in charge of the *Fox* and was to sail it into the islands that stretched from Atlantic to Pacific above the Arctic Circle.

Left: Dr. John Rae. He was a most successful Arctic traveler, borrowing from the early fur traders the habit of making his journeys with little equipment, but in the company of the natives of the region and using the skills they used to survive. He was a superb hunter and could build an igloo or a stone house if necessary. Below: the cutlery that the Eskimos from Pelly Bay gave Rae in 1854. It was Franklin's own, bearing his crest.

On July 1, 1857, a little more than 12 years after John Franklin had sailed on his ill-fated mission, the *Fox* eased from her berth at Aberdeen, Scotland. By the end of the month she had reached Greenland where 35 dogs and an Eskimo were taken on board in preparation for the time when McClintock and his men would abandon their ship for the search over the ice. Early in August they sailed away from Upernavik, the most northern of the Danish settlements in Greenland.

Only 12 days later when attempting to pass from Melville Bay to Lancaster Sound, through vast accumulations of drift-ice, the *Fox* was stopped by the ice and was soon frozen up for the winter. "Then commenced an ice-drift not exceeded in length by any that I know of," wrote McClintock in his journal. "It was not until April 25, 1858, by which time we had drifted down to latitude 63.5°N, that we were able to escape out of the ice, under circumstances which will long be remembered by all on board. A heavy southeast gale rolled in such an ocean-swell that it broke up all the ice, and threw the masses into violent commotion, dashing them one against the other and against the ship in a terrific manner. We owed our escape, under Providence, to the peculiar wedge-formed bow and steam power of our obedient little vessel." In all, the *Fox* had been adrift for 242 days and had been carried 1,194 miles down Baffin Bay to the southeast.

After returning to Greenland for fresh supplies, the *Fox* turned her bow northwestward again. This time, she succeeded in crossing

Above: the *Fox,* the small steamer commanded by Leopold McClintock, which Lady Franklin purchased and outfitted privately. She obtained McClintock's services from the British Navy with the help of Prince Albert. Below: Leopold McClintock. He had already sailed to the Arctic in 1848 as James Clark Ross' second lieutenant.

Melville Bay and reached Pond Inlet on July 27, 1858. McClintock and a small party of men went ashore and visited an Eskimo village at Kaparoktolic. The Eskimo they had taken on board the *Fox* at Greenland acted as McClintock's interpreter and questioned the Eskimos about whether they had seen Franklin or any of his men. They knew nothing about an expedition. This negative reply led McClintock to assume that the *Erebus* and *Terror* must have passed north of Pond's Inlet and the small island to the north of it. He thought they had then made their way through Lancaster Sound into

Right: the departure of exploring parties from the *Fox*. From his service under Ross, McClintock had learned the value of flexibility in approach when in the Arctic, and was quick to use whatever methods might come to hand.

Barrow Strait where they had spent the winter at Beechey Island.

McClintock's next move was to sail the *Fox* to Beechey Island, which he reached in about 10 days. But he found no more clues at Beechey and decided to sail the *Fox* south toward King William Island. When the *Fox* got to Franklin Strait and only 150 miles away from King William Island, the ice again closed in about the tiny ship and held it in a viselike grip. Impatient to continue the search for Franklin, McClintock decided not to wait for the ice to open and made preparations to trek overland with two other men from the *Fox*. On February 17, 1859, accompanied by an Eskimo and a seaman, McClintock started on his way south over the Boothia Peninsula. They had with them two dog sledges to carry supplies. Eleven days later, they met a group of Eskimos who had been hunting near Cape Victoria, 30 miles across the James Ross Strait from King William Island.

Again the Eskimo who was acting as interpreter asked the usual questions about the Franklin expedition. According to McClintock's account, the Eskimos said that several years before, a ship had been crushed by the ice and sunk off the northwestern shore of King William Island. All the men on board had got safely on to land and then went away to a great river where they died. This report confirmed Dr. Rae's discoveries and convinced McClintock that there was nothing more he could do without more men and provisions. So he turned north again and hurried back to the *Fox*.

Above: the chronometer watch that had been issued to the H.M.S. *Terror,* and which McClintock found on the ship's boat. He was appalled at the amount of useless equipment the weakened men had apparently tried to drag on the sledge—even such things as books and silver plate. The sledge weighed nearly three-quarters of a ton.

On April 2, two search parties left the *Fox,* one commanded by McClintock and the other by a Lieutenant Hobson. Both groups covered the icy miles between the *Fox* and Cape Victoria together, but there they separated. McClintock and his men crossed over the ice of James Ross Strait to King William Island and turned south along the east coast of the island. His destination was Back River. Hobson led his sledges over the same ice bridge, but after reaching King William Island, he turned to the west. He would search the northern and western coasts of the island, where according to the Eskimos, the *Erebus* and *Terror* had foundered.

Swiftly, McClintock and his men cut through the ice toward Back River. While still on King William Island, they met about 40 Eskimos who showed them some disturbing souvenirs—silverware bearing the crests and initials of Franklin and some of his officers. When they finally reached Back River however, they found no sign

Right: the sledges approach a point about 12 miles beyond Cape Herschel, where McClintock's party found the letter left by Lieutenant Hobson reporting his discovery of the two notices by the men of Franklin's party.

Franklin (with Back)	1a	1819–22
Franklin (with Back)	1b	1825–7
Franklin (with Crozier)	1c	1845–7
Winter Sledging parties	1D	1847
Crozier (with remaining members of expedition on foot)	1E	1848
● Position of ships in successive winters		

1st. Search expeditions:		
Rae (with Richardson)	2a	1847–9
Ross, James C. (with McClure & McClintock)	2b	1848–9
McClure	2c	1850–5
Collinson	2d	1850–4

2nd. Search expeditions:		
British ships (with Austin, McClintock, John Ross, Ommaney & Penny)	3a	1850–1
Sledging parties from British ships	3b	1851
American ships (with De Haven & Kane)	3c	1850–1
Rae	3d	1850–1

3rd. Search expeditions:		
Rae	4	1853–4

Final Search expeditions:		
McClintock	5a	1857–9
McClintock & sledging parties	5b	1858–9

Right: Northeast Canada and Greenland, showing the routes taken by Sir John Franklin on his three Arctic expeditions. Also shown are the routes of the men who between 1847 and 1859 went to find what had happened to Franklin. They never found him, but their searches added greatly to our detailed knowledge of the Arctic.

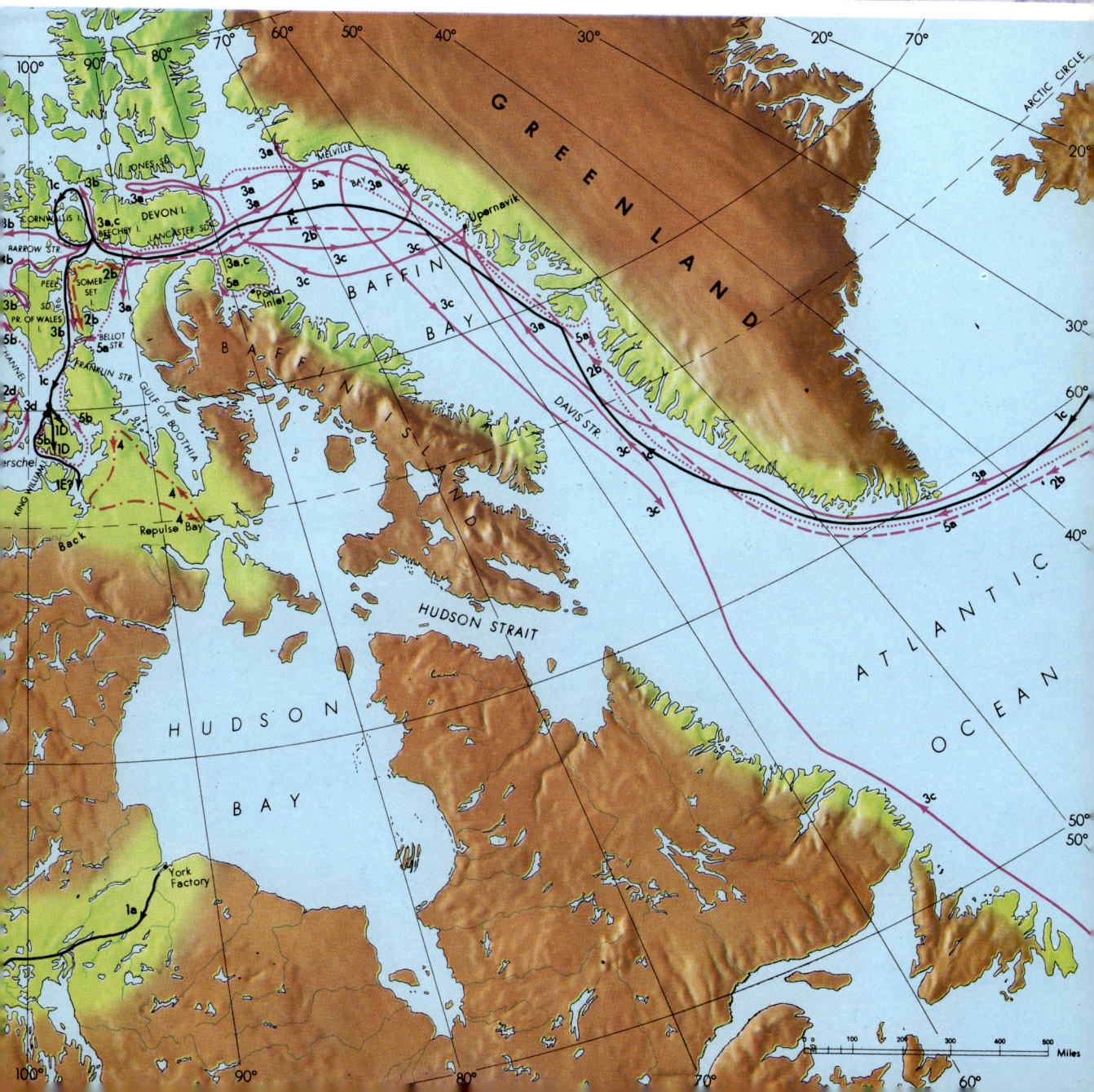

ARCTIC CIRCLE

GREENLAND

BAFFIN BAY

BAFFIN ISLAND

DAVIS STR.

Upernavik

MELVILLE
BAY

JONES SD.

DEVON I.
LANCASTER SD.
BARROW STR.
CORNWALLIS I.
BEECHEY I.

PEEL
SOMER-
SET
PR. OF WALES I.
BELLOT STR.
FRANKLIN STR.

GULF OF BOOTHIA

Pond
Inlet

CHANNEL

KING WILLIAM I.

Herschel

Back

Repulse Bay

HUDSON STRAIT

HUDSON

BAY

York
Factory

ATLANTIC

OCEAN

Miles

of the Franklin mission. Crossing back to King William Island, they headed up the western coast hoping to meet Hobson.

Time was again running out. It was now May, and McClintock knew the *Fox* would have to make its break for England during the early summer thaw. Then at Cape Herschel, on the southwestern coast of King William Island, a "bleached skeleton was found near the beach, around which lay fragments of European clothing. The snow was most carefully removed, and a small pocket-book containing a seaman's parchment certificate and a few letters were found," but still no record of the ill-fated expedition.

A few days later McClintock's party came across the remains of a

28-foot-long ship's boat. It contained two skeletons, some books and old pocket watches, two double-barreled guns, some clothing, supplies of tea and chocolate—but no records. Another perplexing clue was also the fact that the sledge on which the boat was rested was pointing toward the north. Apparently, the men from the *Erebus* and *Terror* had abandoned their ships and headed southward to find one of the outposts of the Hudson's Bay Company. Then for some reason they had turned back in a vain attempt, at least for some, to reach the safety of the ships.

McClintock ordered his sledges to go north, feeling confident he was near the place where the Franklin mystery might be solved. He was also thinking about Hobson's trek around the northwestern coast of King William Island and what his party might have found. In his log McClintock's own words tell us what happened next.

"A few miles beyond Cape Herschel the land becomes very low; many islets and shingle-ridges lie far off the coast; and as we advanced we met with hummocks of unusually heavy ice ... we were approaching a spot where a revelation of intense interest was awaiting .... About 12 miles from Cape Herschel I found a small cairn built by Hobson's search party, and containing a note for me."

On May 6, Hobson had reached Point Victory on the northwest coast of King William Island. While nearing the spit of land that jutted out into Victoria Strait he and his men had spotted a large cairn. Piles of equipment lay around a heap of rocks—cooking stoves, pickaxes, canvas, shovels, and nautical instruments. Then one of Hobson's men came across a rusty cylinder that had apparently been soldered shut at one time only to be reopened and closed again later. What could this mean? When they broke open the cylinder the men found two separately dated notices:

The main entry had been written on May 28, 1847. It read: "H.M. ships *Erebus* and *Terror* wintered in the ice in lat. 70°05′ N., long. 98°23′ W. Having wintered in 1846-7 at Beechey Island, in lat.

Above: Hobson's party smashes open the cairn on Point Victory, to find the record of Crozier and Fitzjames that reported the death of Franklin.

Right: the medicine chest found by Hobson's party with the last written record of the Franklin expedition. It contained pills, ointments, some bandages and oiled silk, and 25 small bottles. It seems odd that it should have been left at the cairn when the surviving expedition members began their doomed march to Back River.

Above: *The Death of Franklin,* by W. Thomas Smith, painted in 1895. The record left by Crozier and Fitzjames stated clearly that Franklin had died before the ships were abandoned, but in this dramatic version the bodies lie around the lifeboat with Franklin the last man alive. This painting was widely exhibited in England, where the public was stunned by the disaster.

74°43′28″ N., long. 91°39′15″ W., after having ascended Wellington Channel to lat. 77°, and returned by the west side of Cornwallis Island. Sir John Franklin commanding the expedition. All well. Party consisting of two officers and six men left the ships on Monday, 24th May, 1847." Signed, Gm. Gore, Lieut. and Chas. F. Des Voeux, Mate.

The marginal entry was written almost a year later: "April 25, 1848—H.M. ships *Terror* and *Erebus* were deserted on the 22nd April, 5 leagues N.N.W. of this, having been beset since 12 Sept., 1846. The officers and crews, consisting of 105 souls, under the command of Captain F. R. M. Crozier, landed here in lat. 69°37′42″ N., long. 98°41′ W. . . . Sir John Franklin died on the 11th June, 1847; and the total loss by deaths in the expedition has been to this date 9 officers and 15 men." Signed, F. R. M. Crozier, Captain and senior officer and James Fitzjames, Captain H.M.S. *Erebus.* There was a final postcript: "and start tomorrow, 26th, for Back's (Great) Fish River."

There was one inconsistency about dates that Hobson had

immediately spotted. The gravestones at Beechey Island bore dates during the winter of 1845–1846. Yet the main entry stated that the *Erebus* and *Terror* wintered at the island in 1846–1847. Hobson concluded that Lieutenant Gore must have made an incorrect entry. The expedition must have spent its first winter on Beechey Island and the second here.

Where had Franklin died? Why hadn't the men joined up with the Eskimos who could have helped them to survive? Why had they been forced back from Back River? For another 20 years parties of explorers would search in vain for the answers.

Right: the last message, written on one of the official printed forms that discovery ships would throw overboard enclosed in bottles to prove the direction of currents. The finder was requested to send it to the Admiralty with a note of the time and the place where it was found.

Below: Fridtjof Nansen's watercolor
of the polar night, November 24, 1893,
He painted it while the *Fram* was
slowly drifting with the pack ice north
of the New Siberian Islands.

The True Viking

5

Ironically it was the failure of one Arctic expedition in 1881 that was to provide a clue to the eventual conquest of the North Geographic Pole. In 1879, Lieutenant George Washington De Long of the United States Navy sailed from San Francisco aboard a ship named the *Jeannette*. But after being underway for only a few months, the *Jeannette* was caught in the ice near Herald Island. Gradually it drifted westward past Wrangel Island and then in a northwesterly direction for 17 months. By June 1881 the *Jeannette* had been crushed in the ice north of the New Siberian Islands. Its crew managed to reach the estuary of the Lena River in Siberia, but hunger and cold killed De Long and all but two of the men. Three years after the *Jeannette* had sunk, some wreckage from the ship was found on the southwest coast of Greenland. How had an old pair of oilskin trousers and the other remnants from the *Jeannette* got from Siberia to southwest Greenland? Had they perhaps drifted across the North Pole or very close to it?

A newspaper article about the mysterious items from the *Jeannette* was read by a young Norwegian explorer, Fridtjof Nansen. He had previously made trips across the Greenland ice pack and had for several years been speculating about the possibility of a new route to the North Pole. The newspaper account about the wreckage confirmed what Nansen already supposed to be true—that the best route to the North Pole lay along the moving highway of ice that stretched from Siberia to Greenland. There was other evidence to support this theory. One of Nansen's colleagues had received from a Greenlander at Godthåb a remarkable piece of wood, which had been found among the driftwood on the coast. It was one of the "throwing sticks," that Eskimos use in hurling their "bird-darts," but altogether unlike those used by the Eskimos on the west coast of Greenland. This stick must have come from the coast of Alaska in the region of the Bering Strait, as that is the place where that particular kind of throwing stick is used. Furthermore, it was ornamented with Chinese glass beads, very much like those that the Alaskan Eskimos obtain from the people who live along the East Siberian Sea.

Nansen had further evidence of the existence of a current that crossed the North Pole. From his previous voyages he knew that the scrub that grows in Greenland is unsuitable for making the boats and sledges that are such essential items in the lives of the Green-

Above: Fridtjof Nansen at Cape Flora in 1896, photographed by Frederick Jackson, whose hut is in the background. Nansen was a young Norwegian explorer who decided to try out a new route to the North Pole, drifting with the transpolar current.

Left: the discovery of the bodies of the crew of the *Jeannette*. The wreckage of the ship drifted across the North Pole to Greenland, which confirmed Nansen's theory that it was possible to travel on the drifting pack ice.

Below: Nansen's cabin in the *Fram*, with his clothing, as it now appears in the Fram Museum in Oslo, Norway.

Left: the *Fram*, now preserved in the Oslo museum. Nansen designed the ship himself. He planned it to be as small and short as possible, with the sides smooth, so that the crushing ice would slide past them. The bows, stern, and keel were all carefully rounded so that the ice could not secure a grip.

Right: the crew of the *Fram* on the deck after the 1893–1896 expedition. Nansen is in the center of the back row. In front of him at the left is Svedrup, the captain, and on his left is Johansen, who was Nansen's partner on the two-year trek across the ice.

landers. Therefore they must have fashioned these things from driftwood collected along the shoreline. But where did that timber come from? A botanist supplied a feasible answer. In the driftwood that reached Greenland there were pieces of Siberian larch and other kinds of wood that must have drifted over the top of the world from Siberia.

Taken together, these bits of evidence led Nansen to conclude that if timbers could drift across the polar region, that drift might also be used by explorers to get to the North Pole. Nansen was contemplating an expedition aboard a boat that would be properly shaped to allow him to slip through the ice. Using the transpolar current he, like the wreckage from the *Jeannette*, could cross the polar basin. Nansen knew that the current might not carry him exactly across the pole, but at least it would enable him to explore the region.

Nansen's next project was the design and construction of a ship that could ride the ice highway without being crushed. He wanted to have a ship built as small and as strong as possible—"just big enough to contain . . . coal and provisions for 12 men for 5 years. The essential factor was that the ship should be able to withstand the pressure of the ice. The sides should slope sufficiently to prevent the ice from getting a firm hold on the hull. . . . Instead of nipping the ship, the ice should raise it up out of the water."

With the money he received from the Norwegian government for the proposed expedition Nansen had a ship designed and built

according to his conceptions. On June 24, 1893, the small but rugged vessel that Nansen christened the *Fram* ("Forward") was ready to sail from Pepperviken, Norway. Aboard it were 12 Norwegians including Nansen and Otto Sverdrup, the captain.

As the expedition got underway Nansen jotted in his diary, "It was midsummer day. A dull, gloomy day; and with it came the inevitable leave-taking. . . . Behind me lay all I held dear in life. And what before me?" For Franklin and De Long the answer had been hardship and death. For Nansen? He knew quite well the risks that lay waiting. "Like an arrow the little boat sped over Lysaker Bay bearing me on the first stage of a journey on which life itself, if not more, was staked."

For the next few months the *Fram* sailed eastward, along the coast of northern Europe and then into the waters of the Arctic Ocean above Russia. Nansen had planned to take on supplies at the New Siberian Islands before beginning the hazardous drive toward the Arctic ice pack. However, he changed direction northward before reaching them and before September was over, the *Fram* was locked in the ice. From then on it would go where the ice took it.

The men on board resigned themselves to the prospect of isolation and wandering for at least the next two years. As winter approached the ice pack grew, and Nansen and his crew began to wonder whether the *Fram*, like the *Jeannette*, might be crushed by it? One black December evening as they were sitting at supper they heard the sound of cracking ice. The cracking sound became a roar so loud that it was impossible for the crew to hear one another's voices. Then the ship began to rise as the ice squeezed against its sides. Nansen's theory about the design of the *Fram* was correct.

Now began a long succession of monotonous days, weeks, and months of drifting as the ice floes drifted. Nansen, who throve on activity, was particularly affected by the confinement. "I long to return to life," he wrote in his diary. "At times this inactivity crushed one's very soul; one's life seems as dark as the winter night outside. . . . I feel as if I must break through this deadness, this inertia, and find some outlet for my energies. Can't something happen? Could not a hurricane come and tear up this ice, and set it rolling in high waves like the open sea?"

By late December the *Fram* had reached latitude 82° 30′ N. No ship, adrift or under its own power, had poked its bow so close to the North Pole. And none had probably encountered the icy pressure ridge that crept threateningly closer and closer to the helpless, ice-locked ship. Nansen writes, "The floe, seven feet thick, has borne down on us on the port side, forcing itself up on the ice in which we are lying, and crushing it down. Thus the *Fram* was forced down with the ice, while the other floe, packed up on the ice beneath, bore down on her, and took her amidships while she was still frozen fast. As far as I can judge, she could hardly have had a tighter squeeze; it was no wonder that she groaned under it;

Above: the *Fram* locked in the ice during the winter of 1894-1895. As the ice closed in, the *Fram* withstood the pressure and drifted with the slow ice flow, confirming Nansen's ideas.

but she withstood it, broke loose and eased." Again, the *Fram* had proved its ice-worthiness.

Although elated by the behavior of the ship, Nansen and his crew continued to become depressed by the frustratingly slow drift of the ice. Moreover, as each day passed, it became apparent that the ice drift would not carry them across the pole. The *Fram's* northward drift had stopped at about 84° N. latitude. It was now being pulled toward the west. Nansen guessed that they would remain locked in the ice for at least a year—and perhaps for two or three years. He also knew that he could not endure the enforced idleness and began to plan how he could get farther north to the pole, which was only 350 miles away.

For a while he had been calculating that two hardy men, equipped with sledge, dog teams, kayaks, and carrying enough food for 100 days could cover the distance in 50 days—if all went well. Nansen decided that he would try to make this journey, accompanied by one of the young officers on the *Fram,* Hjalmar Johansen. He would leave Captain Sverdrup in charge of the ship.

Below: the *Fram* in the ice in July, 1894. Above the awning over the deck is the windmill. It was designed to drive the generator that would produce electric light for the ship, as the ship's engine would not be running once the *Fram* was frozen in.

Below: the Arctic Ocean, showing the ocean currents and ice drift suggested by the observed movement of driftwood and other objects. Nansen was convinced that the Arctic ice drift shown here could be used to carry a ship, locked in the ice, across the Arctic to the North Pole. The course of the *Fram*, in which he set out to prove his theory, is plotted on the map on page 87.

On March 14, 1895, Nansen and Johansen left the *Fram* and set out for the pole. The first few days of the journey were deceptively easy. The men with their 3 sledges, 27 dogs, and 2 kayaks sped across the flat, smooth ice. But where the ice was broken up into immense jagged ridges, they had to struggle over it.

By April 5, Nansen and Johansen had reached latitude 86°2.8′N.— within 272 miles of the pole. But the going had become so difficult that Nansen began to think about turning back. He reconsidered however, and decided they should at least try to reach 87° N.

PACIFIC OCEAN

ALASKA CURRENT

BERING SEA

BERING STR.

NORTH AMERICA

WRANGELL

NEW SIBERIAN IS

ASIA

Direction of surface currents in January
→ Predominantly Cold Currents
→ Predominantly Warm Currents

ARCTIC OCEAN

NORTH POLE

SEVERNAYA ZEMLYA

ELLESMERE I.

BAFFIN ISLAND

FRANZ JOSEF LAND

LABRADOR CURRENT

SPITZBERGEN

GREENLAND

EAST GREENLAND CURRENT

ICELAND

NORTH ATLANTIC CURRENT

EUROPE

ATLANTIC OCEAN

© Geographical Projects

200   400   600   800   1000
Miles

In his diary Nansen recorded his feelings as they pushed on. "Saturday, April 6. Two A.M., −11.4° F. (−24.2°). The ice grew worse and worse. Yesterday it brought me to the verge of despair. . . . I will go on one day longer, however, to see if the ice is really as bad farther northward as it appears to be from the ridge . . . where we are encamped. . . . Lanes, ridges, and endless rough ice, it looks like an endless moraine of ice-blocks; and this continual lifting of the sledges over every irregularity is enough to tire out giants. . . . I am rapidly coming to the conclusion that we are not doing any good here."

Nevertheless, Nansen and Johansen struggled across the almost impenetrable ice for another two days. "Monday, April 8 . . . the ice grew worse and worse and we got no way. Ridge after ridge . . . stretching as far as the horizon. There is not much sense in keeping on longer; we are sacrificing valuable time and doing little. If there be much more such ice between here and [land], we shall, indeed want all the time we have." The Norwegians had managed to get 160 miles farther north than had any explorer before them.

Then began the journey southward to the nearest piece of land, a group of islands called Franz Josef Land. Not long after they had started to go south both men forgot to wind their watches—an oversight that was to make their trek even more difficult. Without an accurate means of measuring time they would be unable to make precise calculations about their position. Nansen and Johansen could do nothing but rely on the compass, even though it might mean that they would end up miles from Franz Josef Land.

As spring began to come to the Arctic, the ice pack became pockmarked with spots of open blue water, over which a thin sheet of

Above: a chalk drawing of the northern light at midnight, by Nansen. He was fascinated by the effects of the light. Below: two of the *Fram* crew members with their meteorological "observatory." They took readings every four hours.

Above: for the first part of their journey after leaving the *Fram* Nansen and Johansen had dog teams. But the conditions became worse, and they had to start killing their dogs one by one to feed those that remained.
Above right: Nansen and Johansen with kayaks on their ski-sledges. It was a real feat of endurance to drag the sledges over the ice ridges.

ice would often form. When the water was clear, the men, dogs, and sledges would cross these stretches of water in the kayaks. But when it was crusted with ice, they had to make long and tiring detours.

Food was running short and the dogs were beginning to gnaw almost anything they came across that might satisfy their hunger. Nansen decided that they would have to kill the weaker dogs and keep the others alive on their meat. Although Nansen and Johansen still had a small supply of dried meat and some other rations for themselves, these would not hold out for long. On May 15, they celebrated Johansen's 28th birthday by drinking hot lime juice and sugar. By June 9, they were so low on food that they had to kill all but three of the dogs.

Now the weather added to the misery of the exhausted men. Wind-whipped sheets of rain lashed down from gray skies for the next few days. Nansen had an attack of painful lumbago, which made traveling impossible. They decided to make camp rather than sap their strength in a vain attempt to make progress. After resting for three days Nansen felt better, and they decided to push on.

Summer brought better luck. One day Johansen spotted a seal and shot it for their first meal of fresh meat since they had left the luxury of the *Fram*. The terrain was easier now, even though the days dragged on with no sight of land.

On August 7, the men reached open water that stretched as far as they could see. They tied the kayaks together, rigged a sail, loaded supplies and sledges, and pushed off into the water. As the strange vessel bobbed along the water, a fine, damp mist engulfed it. A gentle breeze pushed them onward, and when the mist suddenly lifted Nansen and Johansen saw in the distance a group of tiny islands—the northernmost islands of Franz Josef Land.

Soon they stepped out on one of the islands—the first solid land they had walked on for two years. It was already late summer and they decided to find a suitable place to wait out the Arctic winter, which descends in this region in September. They made their camp in a sheltered spot near a high cliff on one of the northern islands· in Franz Josef Land. Ivory gulls, kittiwakes, skuas, and auks wheeled in the sky above. And bears, seals, and walruses made a playground of the nearby rocks. There would be plenty of fresh meat for the winter.

For shelter, Nansen built a sturdy stone hut roofed with walrus hides. Chinks in the walls and roof were made weather-tight with tiny pebbles, bits of moss, and hide. On October 15, the sun set and the long Arctic night descended for the third time on Nansen and Johansen. Occasionally, one of them would go outside to hunt down a meal or repair a part of the hut, but it would be nine months before they would again be able to move on toward Norway. Finally on May 19, 1896, they took one last look at their winter home and put their kayaks into the water.

The next few weeks were full of unexpected adventures—and misadventures. One day, a walrus ripped open the side of Nansen's kayak. Fortunately, he quickly paddled to a spot over a half-submerged piece of ice where he was able to repair the jagged hole. Another time when the men had stopped to go ashore on an island, their kayaks, which had not been moored firmly enough, began to drift away. Nansen's quick thinking in this sort of situation is best described by his diary entry for that day. "We went up to a hummock close by. As we stood there, Johansen suddenly cried, 'I say, the kayaks are adrift!'" Nansen quickly threw off some clothing and plunged into the water. "The water was icy cold; it was hard work swimming with clothes on. . . . But all our hope was drifting there; all we possessed was on board—we had not even a knife with us: and whether I got cramp and sank here, or turned back without the kayaks, it would come to pretty much the same thing." But Nansen

Above: the Aurora Borealis, by Nansen. He wrote of the Arctic night, "It is dreamland, painted in the imagination's most delicate tints; it is colour etherealised. One shade melts into the other, so that you cannot tell where one ends and the other begins." Below: Nansen and Johansen's boat, made by lashing together two kayaks.

did not drown. He caught the kayaks, which were attached to the same line and hoisted himself into one of them and paddled back to Johansen.

Then one morning when the two men had camped temporarily on another of the Franz Josef Land islands, Nansen heard the distant sound of barking. The last of their own dogs had been killed months ago so the sound was not a familiar one. Nansen immediately forgot the breakfast he was cooking and started walking and running in the direction of the barking.

In his diary Nansen described his emotions at this crucial moment. "It was with a strange mixture of feelings that I made my way in towards land among the numerous hummocks. . . . Suddenly I thought I heard a shout from a human voice, a strange voice, the first for three years. How my heart beat and the blood rushed to my brain as I ran up the hummock and hallooed with all the strength of my lungs! . . . Soon I heard another shout, and saw, too, from an ice-ridge, a dark form moving among the hummocks farther in. It was a dog; but farther off came another figure, and that was a man. . . . We approached one another quickly. I waved my hat; he did the same. I heard him speak to the dog, and I listened. It was English, and as I drew nearer I thought I recognized Mr. Jackson [Frederick Jackson, an English Arctic explorer]. . . ." The two men exchanged greetings, almost unable to believe that their meeting was actually happening and was not a dream.

Then less than a month after this chance meeting the *Windward,* one of the ships in Jackson's expedition, arrived at Cape Flora, one of the southern islands of Franz Josef Land. With Nansen and Johansen aboard, the *Windward* weighed anchor and headed toward Norway on August 7. The news that Nansen had been found alive was telegraphed to Norway. When the two explorers, whom many had thought were dead, arrived in Norway they at last got word about the *Fram,* which had sailed into the port of Skjaervo, Norway on August 20. After drifting for 35 months it had broken out of the ice northwest of Spitzbergen. Not a single man had been lost and the *Fram,* having sustained the battering of the ice, at last set sail for Norway, which it had left more than three years before.

Thus ended one of the greatest Arctic journeys, organized in a scientific way and led by an exceptional man of imagination and intelligence. Although Nansen and Johansen never reached the North Pole they did get to within 272 miles of it. Their observations about the polar region, and those carried out by the *Fram* as it drifted along with the ice were to give future Arctic explorers a basis from which to carry out their work.

Nansen lived and worked during a period when the Scandinavian countries were once again exerting their almost instinctive urge to explore and to cross the unknown world. This impulse can be said to be part of the national heritage that men like Nansen inherited from their Viking ancestors.

Right: the historic meeting of Nansen and Frederick Jackson. Jackson greeted him cordially, but obviously did not recognize him at first. Then he peered at him intently, asked "Aren't you Nansen?" and when Nansen said that he was, seized his hand thankfully and said, "By Jove! I am glad to see you!"

Below: crew members who remained on the *Fram*, celebrating a Norwegian holiday in May, 1896. The *Fram* at last broke loose from the ice after 35 months, northwest of Spitzbergen.

Reaching the North Pole

6

Ten years after his attempt to drift across the polar region, Fridtjof Nansen was asked by the United States President Theodore Roosevelt to recommend the best American explorer to lead an expedition to the North Pole. At that time there were numerous explorers from many countries striving to reach the North Pole, and to Nansen's experienced eye Robert E. Peary, a young naval officer, seemed the most likely one to win the competition.

In 1886, Peary had made the first of many expeditions to Greenland and already he was obsessed by an overriding ambition to conquer the Artic's great geographical prize. Even though Nansen had discovered that the polar region was an ice-covered sea, Peary still wanted to be the first man to get to the North Pole. Unlike the Norwegian, scientific exploration was not his primary aim. He was a naval officer, who considered his attempt on the pole in terms of the tactics and strategy of getting there. Peary's 1886 crossing of the Greenland ice sheet and his subsequent Greenland journeys were really training exercises. Above all he wanted to prove that he could conquer the Arctic. To do this he must rigorously prepare himself and test all kinds of equipment before trying for the pole.

In May, 1893, Peary was again in Greenland. He and one companion drove forward into the icy wasteland. Through swirling snow

Left: the taffeta flag made by Peary's wife, which he took to the North Pole. Peary wore it wrapped around his body, not trusting it to a sledge, and when he reached each expedition's objective would cut a small piece of the flag and bury it at that point. In 1909, when he reached the North Pole, and after the photographs had been taken, he cut a four-inch diagonal strip from the center and buried that.

Right: Robert E. Peary on the *Roosevelt* after his epic achievement. His face is worn and weary with the fatigue of the 1,000 miles he had sledged.

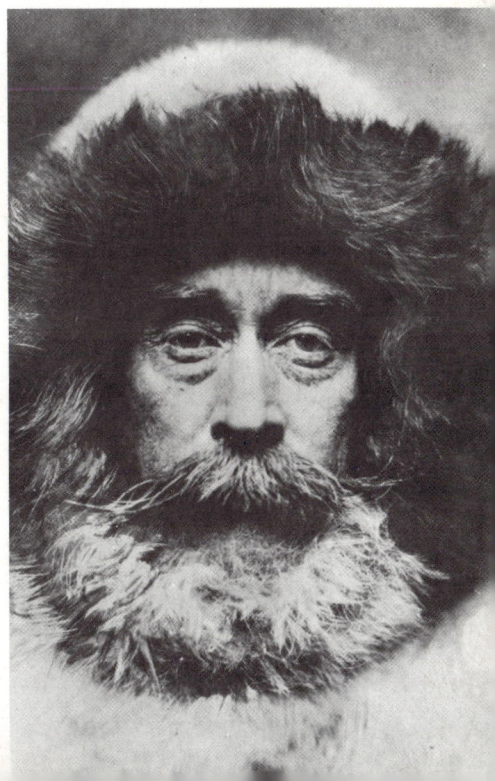

and stinging wind the men struggled forward until they reached the northeast coast of Greenland. This crossing convinced Peary he could get to the North Pole, but not with a large expedition. Only a few men should make the final dash from the base camp.

In the years between 1893 and 1897 Robert Peary spent most of his time in Greenland, striking northward in hopes of finding a suitable place for an advanced base camp that could someday be used for the last crucial phase of getting to the North Pole. These forays into the Greenland ice made him realize, however, that Greenland was not the right place for an advanced camp. The reason

Above: members of Peary's expedition taking a dog team across a lead on a floating cake of ice. One of the constantly recurring problems of Peary's attempts to reach the North Pole was the opening and closing leads. Below: an aerial view of a lead in the ice. These long, narrow water passages through the pack ice constantly shift in position, opening and closing without warning. A hazard of polar bivouacs has always been the possibility of a lead opening at night and carrying away the sleeping men.

for discarding a Greenland route was the comparatively rapid movement of ice in this region as it swung around the northern coast of the island and into the southerly East Greenland Current.

During a trip in 1902, Peary switched his starting point to Grant Land (on the northern edge of Ellesmere Island). The condition of the ice was very bad, and by mid-April he had managed to get only as far north as latitude 84°17′27″. Early in April, at Cape Hecla, he had left land behind him, hoping this time to get across the pack ice to the pole. In parts the snow covering the pack was so soft that the dogs wallowed in it up to their bellies. Very frequently Peary and his companions were forced to double in their tracks and to make exhausting detours to find smoother ground. Then a blizzard caused the pack ice to move, and two wide channels of water opened up across their path.

Even though this journey of 1902 was one more failure for Peary, it had not been entirely unprofitable. The expedition had laid a number of advance depots along this new route to the North Pole, and Peary had learned several invaluable things about the ice pack. Even here, far to the west of the East Greenland Current, the prevailing drift of the ice was from west to east. In order to offset this drift and reach the pole a course of NNW would have to be set. Another lesson Peary had learned was that a rapid return from the North Pole would have to be made if he was to be able to follow the line of his track northward. There were improvements that could also be made in equipment and in the tactics of the assault. Sledges would have to be lighter to ride easily over the hummocky ice and they should also be wider to bridge channels and water leads. Furthermore, a ship would have to be found to penetrate through Smith Sound to the edge of the polar sea, thus reducing the long journey to the advance base camp. From there an advance party would be needed to push on ahead and break a trail. The final

Below: Peary on board the *Roosevelt*, the ship especially built for his 1905 expedition.

assault party for the North Pole would then pass the advance group and thus conserve their energies for the ultimate race to their goal.

In 1902, Peary returned to the United States having spent four years in the Arctic. He devoted himself to the task of raising money for a new expedition that would incorporate his ideas about new equipment and tactics. A group of wealthy New Yorkers formed an organization called the Peary Arctic Club, and by 1904 they had raised enough money for a new ship to be designed and built.

Then in July, 1905, Peary, who was now 50 and had spent nearly 20 years of his life exploring the Arctic, took another crack at the "impossible." His new ship, the *Roosevelt,* which had been especially designed and built to penetrate the ice of Smith Sound, made its way to Greenland where Eskimos and Siberian huskies were taken aboard. The Eskimos would drive the dog teams and build igloos that would be used as supply camps along the route. Eskimo women were taken on to sew clothing for Peary and the six other men in the expedition—the same kind of outfits that the Eskimos fashioned for themselves from the hides of seals and walruses. Peary's respect for the Eskimos' methods of travel and technique of survival was a significant aspect of his eventual success.

The *Roosevelt* battered its way through the ice to Cape Columbia on the northeast coast of Grant Land. Now the expedition was within 90 miles of the advance base camp at Cape Hecla. The first party of Eskimos started out over the ice in February, 1906. Peary's strategy, as explained earlier, was for these advance parties to blaze the trail and establish supply stations along the route, enabling Peary to take a small party of rested men and dogs for the final dash to the pole.

After so many years of planning and careful thought, it seemed only fair that this time Robert Peary would get to the North Pole. But again conditions were unfavorable and temperatures dropped to a record low of −60°F. The bad surface on the ice and the drift of the floe were also against success. Their rate of speed was reduced to five miles a day, and because of this provisions would never hold out for the journey to the North Pole and back. Peary realized that once again he would fail to attain his goal. To help compensate for another failure he decided to push on north until he got as far as any other explorer had. He discarded every possible inessential item from his sledges and with the least exhausted of the dogs plunged on until he got to latitude 87°6′—a new high latitude in the Arctic.

The *Roosevelt* returned to New York with Peary still feeling that he would somehow conquer the North Pole. He soon began organizing a new expedition and in July, 1908, Peary again set out with the *Roosevelt.* The same Britisher, Captain Bob Bartlett, again navigated the ship, and also on board was Peary's devoted servant, Matthew Henson.

The *Roosevelt* docked at Etah, in Greenland, where 50 Eskimos and 250 dogs were engaged for the expedition. By early September

Right: a photograph by Peary of the dog teams walking across the bumpy ridges of the ice hummocks at the beginning of the expedition's march from Cape Columbia. Throughout the winter advance parties stocked the depots on the way to the North Pole.

Left: the expedition moving across the ice, by F. W. Stokes, who went with Peary to the Arctic. The sledges had to travel across the vast, featureless expanses, where each mile looked much like the last, with only the changing pattern of ice ridges or the challenge of the leads opening before them to break the monotonous sameness of the trek through the icy cold of dark days.

Right: a bear walking in the Arctic under the strange brilliant colors of the polar light, by F. W. Stokes.

Captain Bartlett had maneuvered the ship to Cape Sheridan on the Ellesmere coast. During the autumn all the supplies that would be needed for the spring drive to the pole were taken to the advance base at Cape Columbia. By the end of February, 1909, Peary was ready to move over the ice to the North Pole.

Peary describes his feelings on the day he had chosen to start the assault, which was March 1. "When I awoke before light on the morning of March 1, the wind was whistling around the igloo. . . . I looked through the peephole of the igloo and saw that the weather was still clear, and that the stars were scintillating like diamonds. . . . After breakfast, with the first glimmer of daylight, we got outside the igloo and looked about . . . the ice fields to the north, as well as all the lower part of the land, were invisible in that gray haze which, every experienced Arctic traveler knows, means vicious wind. . . . Some parties would have considered the weather impossible for traveling . . . (but) we were all in our new and perfectly dry fur clothes and could bid defiance to the wind.

"One by one the divisions drew out from the main army of sledges and dog teams, took up Bartlett's trail over the ice and disappeared to the northward in the wind haze." (Captain Bartlett, master of the *Roosevelt,* had left Cape Columbia the day before with sledges, dogs, and provisions, as part of Peary's plan of having various support parties in his advance on the Pole.)

Peary's own party, which was the last to leave camp, consisted of 24 men, 19 sledges, and 133 dogs. Their goal was the almost mystical figure of 90°N. latitude, 420 nautical miles to the north.

Peary's party ran into trouble on their second day out. Toward afternoon, Peary "saw ahead of us a dark ominous cloud upon the northern horizon, which always means open water . . . the open water supplies the evaporation, the cold air acts as a condenser, and when the wind is blowing just right this forms a fog so dense that at times it looks as black as the smoke of a prairie fire." Then the party had to stop suddenly to avoid a yawning, quarter-of-a-mile-wide lead that had formed. Peary ordered the men to camp, hoping that if they waited the ice would come together again.

Before dawn the next morning they were awakened by the screech of grinding ice. The lead was closing. After a hurried breakfast, the party set out across the ice, "which was moving

Above: the "home stretch" of Peary's race to the North Pole, showing the weary men hauling the sledges over pressure ridges that could sometimes be as high as 50 feet. Peary is in the center, and the man holding the dogs is his companion, Matthew Henson.

Right: The Arctic Ocean, showing the routes of explorers from De Long in the 1880's, through Peary's successful expedition to the North Pole in 1908–1909, to Wally Herbert and the British Trans-Arctic Expedition in 1968–1969.

© Geographical Project

Legend:

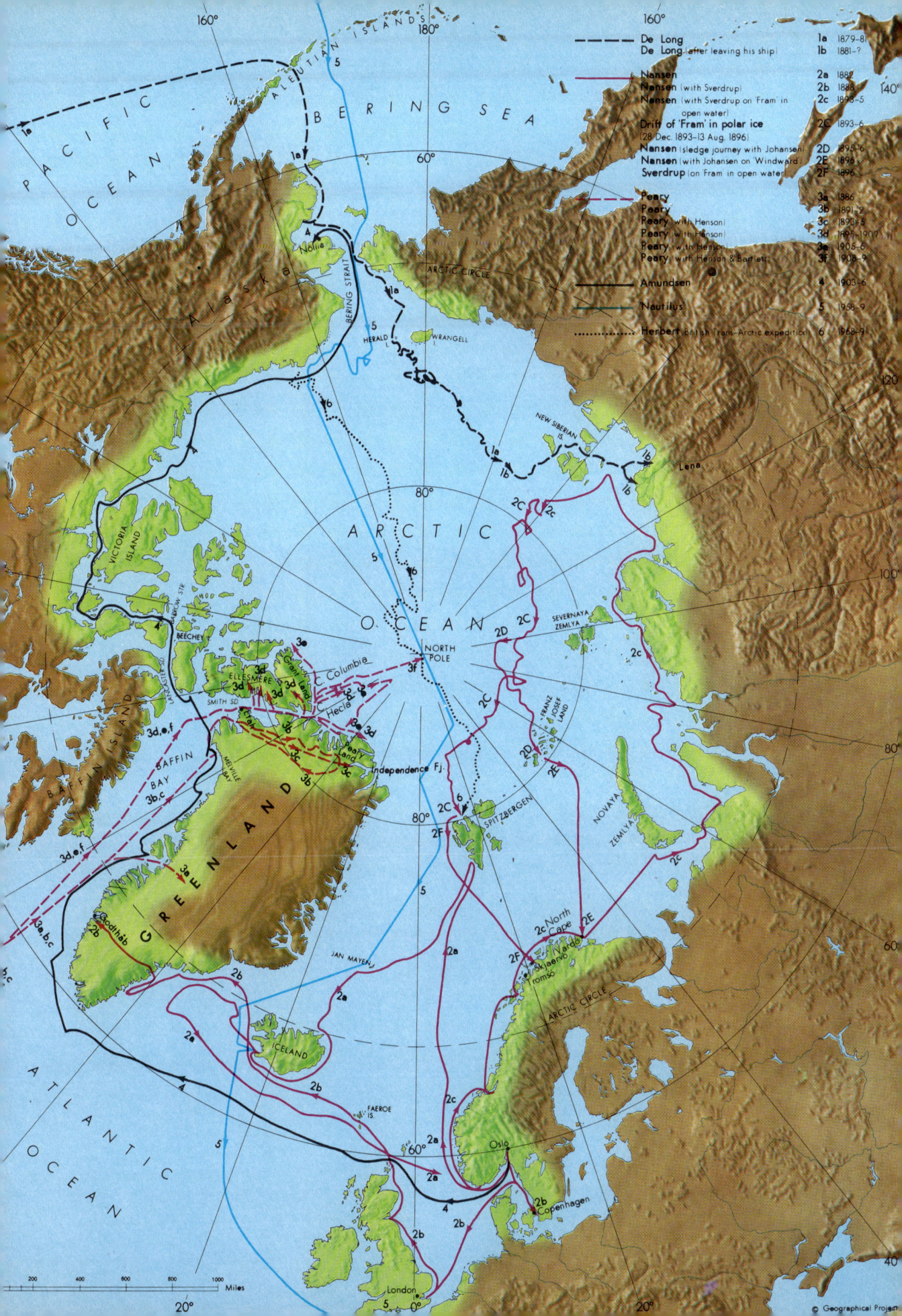

Expedition	Code	Dates
De Long	1a	1879–81
De Long (after leaving his ship)	1b	1881–?
Nansen (with Sverdrup)	2a	1882
Nansen (with Sverdrup)	2b	1888
Nansen (with Sverdrup on 'Fram' in open water)	2c	1893–5
Drift of 'Fram' in polar ice (28 Dec. 1893–13 Aug. 1896)	2C	1893–6
Nansen (sledge journey with Johansen)	2D	1895–6
Nansen (with Johansen on Windward)	2E	1896
Sverdrup (on Fram in open water)	2F	1896
Peary	3a	1886
Peary (with Henson)	3b	1891–2
Peary (with Henson)	3c	1893–5
Peary (with Henson)	3d	1895–1902
Peary (with Henson)	3e	1905–6
Peary (with Henson & Bartlett)	3f	1908–9
Amundsen	4	1903–6
Nautilus	5	1958–9
Herbert British Trans-Arctic expedition	6	1968–9

Map labels:

PACIFIC OCEAN
BERING SEA
ALEUTIAN ISLANDS
ARCTIC OCEAN
ATLANTIC OCEAN
ALASKA
Nome
BERING STRAIT
HERALD
WRANGELL
ARCTIC CIRCLE
NEW SIBERIAN IS.
Lena
NORTH POLE
VICTORIA ISLAND
M'CLURE STR.
BEECHEY
BAFFIN ISLAND
BAFFIN BAY
LANCASTER SD.
MELVILLE BAY
ELLESMERE IS.
Grant Land
SMITH SD.
C. Columbia
Hecla
Peary Land
Independence Fj.
GREENLAND
Godthåb
SEVERNAYA ZEMLYA
FRANZ JOSEF LAND
NOVAYA ZEMLYA
SPITZBERGEN
North Cape
Vardø
Skjærvø
Tromsø
Oslo
Copenhagen
JAN MAYEN
ICELAND
FAEROE IS.
London

Scale: 200 400 600 800 1000 Miles

THE NEW YORK HERALD.

NEW YORK, TUESDAY, SEPTEMBER 7, 1909.—TWENTY FOUR PAGES.

ROBERT E. PEARY, AFTER 23 YEARS SIEGE, REACHES NORTH POLE; ADDS "THE BIG NAIL" TO NEW YORK YACHT CLUB'S TROPHIES; DR. COOK TO SUBMIT RECORDS TO UNIVERSITY OF DENMARK

Discoverer of the Pole Joins in Cheering When Told Mr. Peary's Success

"If He Has Announced He Has Reached the Farthest North, He Has," Is the Physician's First Comment.

"THERE IS HONOR ENOUGH ON IT FOR BOTH OF US," HE ASSERTS TO ADMIRERS

Attains Highest Point on April 6, 1909, Year After Dr. Cook's Discovery

Sends First News of His Achievement from Indian Harbor via Cape Ray, on Newfoundland Coast.

FILES MESSAGES OF SUCCESS, THEN SPEEDS AWAY FOR HOME COUNTRY

Mr. E. H. Harriman Suffers Setback from Indigestion

MISS STEWART IS MADE A PRINCESS

DR. COOK CONGRATULATES MR. PEARY

Left: the front page of the New York Herald, *September 7, 1909, reporting that Peary had reached the North Pole. It was not until five months after his triumph that the news finally reached the United States.*

Below: Peary's photograph of his team standing at the North Pole beneath the flag his wife had made. From left to right, they are Ooqueah, Ootah, Matthew Henson, Egingwah, and Seegloo. After the picture, Peary buried a strip cut from the flag.

crushing, and piling up." It was extremely rough going. The sledges were "crossing a river on a succession of gigantic [ice] shingles, one, two, or three feet deep and all afloat and moving." Peary was afraid that, at any moment, one of the sledges would disappear into the icy water, but none did.

Then, after Peary had caught up with Bob Bartlett's advance party, they found themselves stopped again because of a huge lead. This time Peary waited for a week for the lead to freeze over. Then for almost three weeks Peary and various supporting parties plunged ahead. After they had set up supply camps along the route, the supporting groups would one by one make their way back to Cape Columbia, leaving the two most rested groups—Peary's and Bartlett's—to make the dash for the North Pole. When it came time to decide who would go, Peary was the man to lead the party that consisted of 4 Eskimos and Matthew Henson. They had 5 sledges and 40 dogs for the final assault that began on April 2.

In 5 forced marches Peary drove his party over the final 133 miles to the North Pole. By noon of April 6, 1909, they reached the latitude of 89°57′N., just 3 miles south of their goal.

The story of the rest of their journey is one of the greatest success stories of man against the elements of nature. Although exhausted by the strain of the forced marches, Peary managed to use that final spurt of energy to lead his men to the pole and the prize of 300 years of Arctic exploration. There they camped for 30 hours before beginning their race southward back to Cape Columbia. By pushing on to the North Pole and then returning safely to the *Roosevelt,* Robert Peary had proved that it was possible for men to walk 900 miles over the drifting ice floes of the Polar Sea to the spot in the Northern Hemisphere that is farthest from the equator.

Roald Amundsen (1872–1928)   Robert Falcon Scott (1868–1912)

Two men who raced for the South Pole. Below left: Amundsen of Norway. He was the son of a shipowner, and had trained himself for exploration, studying navigation and seamanship. He was the first man to sail through the Northwest Passage and had hoped to be the first at the North Pole. Below: Scott of England, in a photograph taken on October 7, 1911, in his den at McMurdo Sound with pictures of his wife and son. He left on his final journey on November 1.

Duel for the South Pole

7

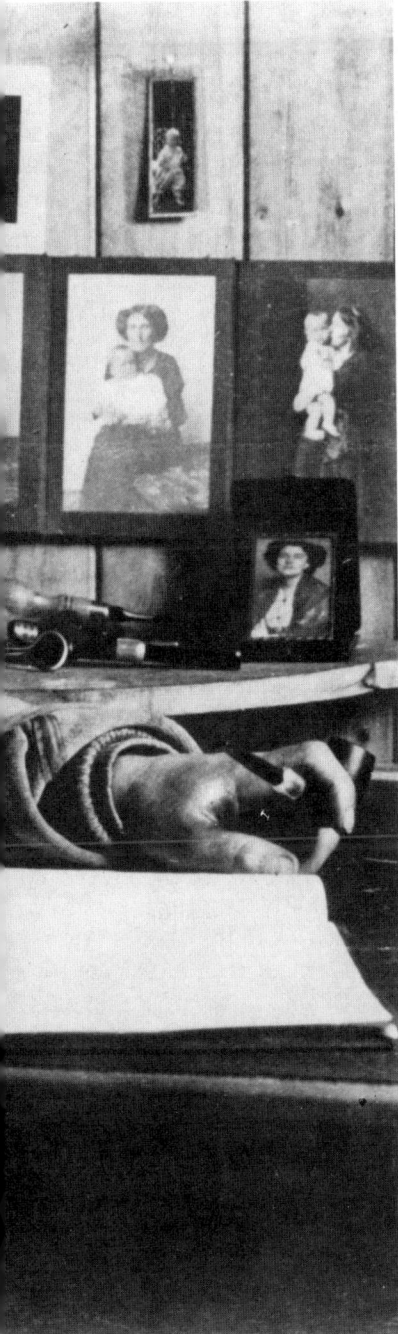

The South Pole is the geographical bottom of the world, 90° south of the equator where all the meridians of longitude come together. Located on the flat, featureless plateau that caps the Antarctic continent, it can only be found by precise astronomical observations. The South Pole cannot otherwise be identified from any other spot on the vast snowfield. Today it is no more than a curiosity, a place for visiting scientists to fly across to say that they have been there. Yet to be the first to reach this icy, undistinguished dot on the map, men suffered incredible privation, showed indomitable courage, and left their frozen bodies to mark the place where, in the end, they failed.

In 1908, an Irishman named Ernest Shackleton led a British expedition to within 97 miles of the pole when lack of food and the approaching Antarctic winter forced him to turn back. It was to be a matter of only a few months before two explorers—Roald Amundsen of Norway and the Englishman Robert F. Scott—were to begin their dramatic race to be first at the pole.

These two men were strikingly different people. As a young naval cadet, Scott was called "old mooney" because of his constant daydreaming. His teachers despaired of his laziness, his slovenly appearance, his uncontrollable temper. As an adult, he was a hard taskmaster and disciplinarian who, despite weak lungs and a less than powerful physique, drove himself harder than he drove his men. He was also a sentimentalist who cried when he heard old hymns, and who could not bear to see a sledge dog killed. He was a brilliant, moody, brave, and iron-willed man who set off for the South Pole at the age of 42.

Amundsen was a simpler and more direct person. Fascinated from boyhood by Sir John Franklin's quest for the Northwest Passage, and by the tales of the expeditions that went to look for the missing Franklin mission, Amundsen was determined to explore the Arctic. Although he had studied to be a medical doctor, at the age of 21 he gave up medicine and began preparing himself for a career as an explorer. He served as a seaman aboard an Arctic merchant vessel and then signed on as first mate aboard the Antarctic-bound *Belgica,* the first ship to spend a winter there. Upon his return to Norway Amundsen bought the 45-foot *Gjoa,* and in a year and eight months managed to make his way through the legendary Northwest Passage. While Scott became a polar explorer comparatively late in

life, Amundsen had always known what he wanted to do. His polar experience, skill in planning expeditions, and raw courage were second to none.

After his triumph in the *Gjoa*, Amundsen turned immediately toward his other goal—the North Pole itself. It was not long before he announced his plans for a drifting expedition in Nansen's famous *Fram* across the pole. But funds for even the famous Amundsen were only reluctantly forthcoming from the Norwegian government, and valuable time was slipping away. While the expedition was still in its planning stages, the news that Peary had reached the North Pole flashed around the world in September, 1909. The prize that Amundsen had wanted for himself had been won by someone else. The Norwegian, however, continued to plan for his drift over the pole—or so he claimed.

During the years when Amundsen had been taking the *Gjoa* through the Northwest Passage, Robert Scott had led an expedition to the Antarctic and had managed to get to within 575 miles of the South Pole. He had returned to England a hero, and in 1909 announced his plans to conquer the pole. The ship he selected for the expedition was an old whaler called the *Terra Nova*. Among the men chosen by Scott to accompany him there were half a dozen scientists who would carry out their particular scientific observations in Antarctica. Because he had been disappointed with the performance of the sledge dogs on the previous trip, Scott took aboard the *Terra Nova* 19 sturdy Siberian ponies that he would use to haul supplies for part of the journey to the pole. On June 1,

Above left: the Scott expedition ship, the *Terra Nova,* caught in the pack ice that delayed the party on the journey to McMurdo Sound in 1910.

Above: December 17, 1910 in the wardroom of the *Terra Nova.* By this time the men on board knew that Amundsen had changed his objective to the South Pole, and the race was on. Scott is sitting at the head of the table.

Right: Fridtjof Nansen's famous ship, the *Fram,* in which Amundsen first planned to drift across the North Pole. After the news of Peary's success reached him, he took the ship south to race Scott to the South Pole.

1910, the *Terra Nova* sailed from London and made its way south-eastward to New Zealand.

Two months later Roald Amundsen headed south—his apparent goal Cape Horn and the Pacific gateway to the Arctic Ocean. But, secretly, he had changed his plans and had decided to try for the South Pole. Not until September 9, at Funchal in the Madeira Islands, did he reveal his real plan to the members of his expedition. Scott was not then in New Zealand, but when the *Terra Nova* docked there in October, Scott received this terse cable that Amundsen had sent from Madeira: "BEG LEAVE TO INFORM YOU PROCEEDING ANTARCTICA." When the men on the *Terra Nova* heard this news they were indignant. The race for the South Pole was on.

Scott encountered great difficulties with the pack ice in reaching his old camp on McMurdo Sound at the eastern edge of the Ross Ice Shelf. While the camp was being resupplied, the *Terra Nova* skirted eastward along the great wall of ice to the Bay of Whales. There, Scott's worst fears were confirmed. Amundsen had apparently found the going easy in the *Fram,* which was securely anchored off the ice cliffs of the Bay of Whales. This was a disturbing discovery to the men on board the *Terra Nova*—Amundsen was 60 miles nearer the pole than their camp in McMurdo Sound.

Starting out in October, 1911, Amundsen with his 4 companions,

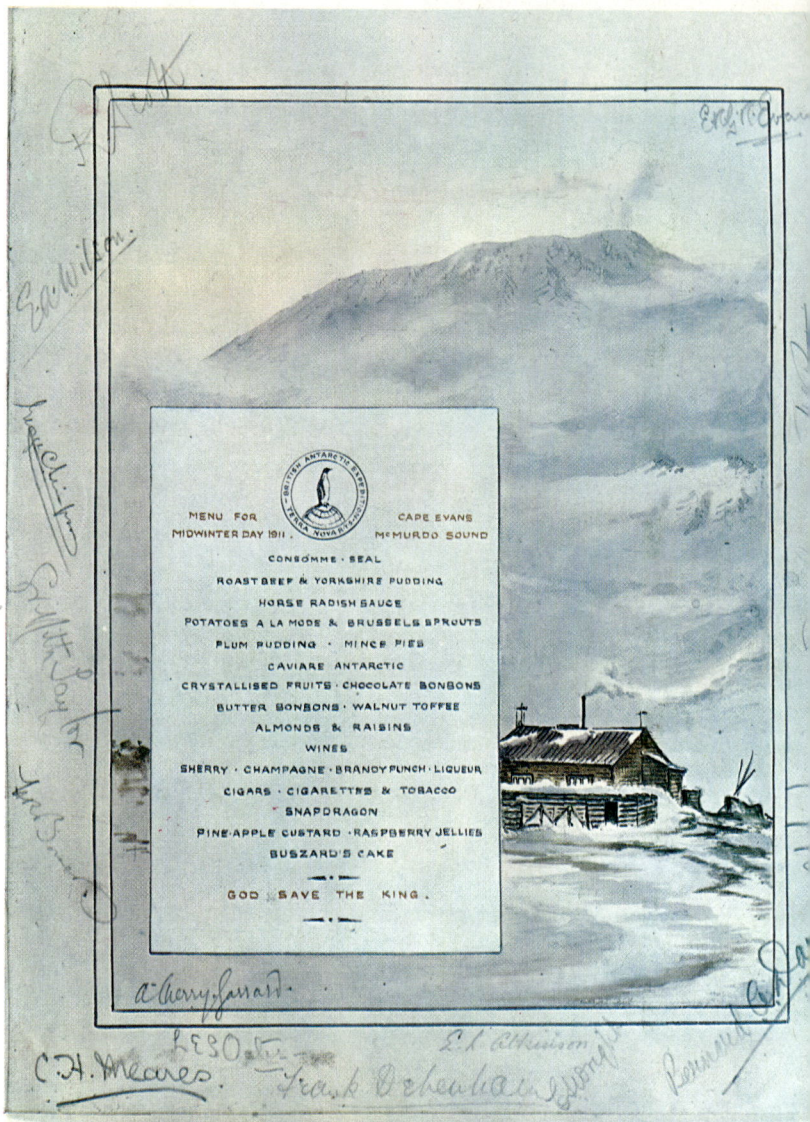

MENU FOR — CAPE EVANS
MIDWINTER DAY 1911. — McMURDO SOUND

CONSOMMÉ · SEAL

ROAST BEEF & YORKSHIRE PUDDING

HORSE RADISH SAUCE

POTATOES A LA MODE & BRUSSELS SPROUTS

PLUM PUDDING · MINCE PIES

CAVIARE ANTARCTIC

CRYSTALLISED FRUITS · CHOCOLATE BONBONS

BUTTER BONBONS · WALNUT TOFFEE

ALMONDS & RAISINS

WINES

SHERRY · CHAMPAGNE · BRANDY PUNCH · LIQUEUR

CIGARS · CIGARETTES & TOBACCO

SNAPDRAGON

PINE-APPLE CUSTARD · RASPBERRY JELLIES

BUZZARD'S CAKE

GOD SAVE THE KING.

Above: "Christmas" celebrations in the Antarctic. The seasons are reversed in the Southern Hemisphere, and Scott and his men celebrated their Christmas in the middle of the polar night on June 22, 1911. It was two months since the sun had gone down. They made a Christmas tree from sticks and skua-gull feathers, and decorated it with colored paper, flags, and presents.

Above right: the Christmas menu. It includes such diverse delicacies as Caviare Antarctica and Buzzard's Cake. Bordering the menu can be seen the signatures of the expedition members.

4 sledges, and 52 dogs reached their southernmost supply depot on November 3. Scott and his companions left McMurdo Sound on November 1. Amundsen was equipped with Siberian huskies and sledges that he had cleverly managed to reduce in weight from 165 pounds each to only 48. Scott was burdened with the heavy ponies who had already shown that they suffered acutely from the cold and the fine snow that drifted through their shaggy coats. Amundsen was entirely preoccupied with reaching the pole. This ambition was made more pressing because of his fear that, as in the Arctic, he might be yet again forestalled. Scott's situation was somewhat different. The scientists in his party planned to carry out their scientific studies of the Antarctic as they went toward the pole.

Amundsen's greatest advantage was that he knew how to dress himself and his men so that they would be lightly and warmly clad. When he had wintered in the Arctic during the period when he was navigating the Northwest Passage he had adopted the Eskimos' way of dressing in loose-fitting garments made of fur. Thus Amundsen and his companions were warmer in their flexible 10-pound suits than the British expedition would ever be in their specially designed outfits that were of double that weight and that would not stay dry. Another thing that proved very helpful to Amundsen were his excellent dogs, which he had purchased in Greenland and that had arrived in the Antarctic in as good a condition as they were when they left home. Furthermore, Amundsen's men knew how to use the dogs and get them to move along quickly with the sledges. The frisky dogs and light sledges covered 90 miles during the first four days after leaving their main camp at the Bay of Whales. After a two-day rest at the first food depot Amundsen pressed ahead.

On leaving the advance depot at 80° south Amundsen put on skis, fixed a rope to one of the sledges and let himself be pulled along. "And there I stood until we reached 85°05′ S.—340 miles. Yes, that was a pleasant surprise. We had never dreamed of driving on skis to the Pole." They were then only 270 miles away from their goal, and it was only the middle of November. There was plenty of time left for the final stages of the push to the pole.

Scott, who had left his camp after Amundsen had set out from his, found the going across the Ross Ice Shelf slower than expected. Because of a summer blizzard from December 4 to December 9, it was impossible to move at all. When they were finally able to continue, the ponies began to sink up to their bellies in the snow and the men were forced to drive them mercilessly. After 15 hours of very slow progress, Scott had to order that the few remaining animals to survive the cold and exposure be shot.

By this time, all the supplies for the final push to the pole had been brought to the foot of the Beardmore Glacier, a vast river of ice flowing down from the upper plateau. But the four-day layover due to the blizzard had cost Scott dearly. Now he was racing both Amundsen and the on-coming Antarctic winter. He remembered that Ernest Shackleton had returned on February 28, 1909, from his attempt at the pole with barely a day to spare before winter locked the continent in its icy grip. And as he reached the foot of the glacier Scott knew that he was behind Shackleton's schedule.

Amundsen, unable to find a broad avenue like the Beardmore

The interior of Discovery Hut, the last permanent base of the Scott expedition. The stores look exactly as they were left 60 years ago, preserved by the low temperatures of the Antarctic.

Glacier, to the upper plateau that stretches on to the South Pole, was forced to climb a narrow ice tongue he named the Axel Heiberg Glacier. It was here that he had underestimated the difficulties and distances of the journey. The snow was so deep and loose that the dogs had trouble finding their footing. Repeatedly Amundsen was forced to turn back and find a new route when his way was barred by massive blocks of ice. He was still nevertheless well ahead of Scott. The men in the British expedition were now man-hauling their sledges up the glacier, and on December 22, they established their upper Glacier Depot at an altitude of 8,000 feet. Already the men were showing signs of acute fatigue, and they were less than half way to the pole.

On December 7, Amundsen and his men reached 88° 23', which had been Shackleton's farthest south point in 1909. To commemorate this achievement Amundsen ordered that the Norwegian flag should be hoisted above one of the sledges. In his book *South Pole,* Amundsen later described his feelings on this occasion. "All the sledges had stopped, and from the foremost of them the Norwegian flag was flying. It shook itself out, waved and flapped so that the silk rustled; it looked wonderfully well in the pure, clear air and the shining white surroundings. . . . No other moment in the whole trip affected me like this. The tears forced their way to my eyes; by no effort of will could I keep them back. Luckily I was some way in advance of the others so that I had time to pull myself together and master my feelings before reaching my comrades."

Just a week later, the Norwegians were at the South Pole. They had camped on December 13 only 15 miles away from it. That night Amundsen was awake off and on "and had the same feeling that I can remember as a little boy of the night before Christmas Eve—an intense expectation of what was going to happen." The next day, the weather was sparklingly clear and by 3 P.M. in the afternoon, they were at 90°S.—the bottom of the world.

Again the Norwegian flag was put up—this time on top of the tent that they planned to leave at the Pole. The men celebrated and gave themselves extra rations. To be certain that they had actually touched the pole itself, they made a $12\frac{1}{2}$ mile circular trek around their camp. Then, on December 17, 1911, they started back to Framheim.

On New Year's Day, 1912, Scott wrote optimistically in his

journal: "Only 170 miles to the Pole and plenty of food." Three days later as he prepared for the final dash he added a fifth man to the group already chosen. The inclusion of one more man was perhaps Scott's most misguided decision, made at a time when he was too absorbed in his ambition to reach the pole to be able to think clearly. The addition of Lieutenant Bowers would mean overcrowding the tent and disorganizing a well-planned routine. Everything was ready—tent, food, and equipment—but of course this meant everything for four men and not five. There was also the matter of skis. Bowers had left his skis behind at the foot of the

Above: a photograph by Scott of his sledge teams drawn by Siberian ponies. Amundsen's attitude toward his animals was strictly matter-of-fact, they were simply part of the expedition supplies. Scott was sentimental, and could not bear the thought of killing and eating dogs that had helped him haul sledges. The ponies that he took instead were completely unsuitable for the journey. Below: a drawing by Dr. Edward Wilson of two of the ponies in a storm. After the ponies had died, the men of the expedition had to man-haul the sledges.

Right: Antarctica, showing the routes of explorers from 1900 to 1931.

Below: Amundsen's expedition members under the Norwegian flag at the South Pole, December 14, 1911. They made the return trip from the pole easily. With plenty of food and the elation of their triumph to keep them going, they reached their home base on January 25, having made the round trip to the pole in 99 days.

glacier, and he would have to trudge along on foot while the others used skis.

Then there were more blizzards. Soft fields of snow made hauling the sledge an agony, and they could cover no more than 10 miles a day. But Scott would not be disillusioned and remained confident that they would be first at the pole. On January 15 he wrote in his journal: "It is wonderful to see that two long marches will land us at the Pole . . . it ought to be a certain thing now, and the only appalling possibility is the sight of the Norwegian flag forestalling ours."

After that date, however, his journal entries became grim and heartrending. "We started off in high spirits in the afternoon, feeling that tomorrow would see us at our destination. About the

98

Scott (with Shackleton, Wilson & Wild)	1a	1900-4
Scott (with Wilson & Priestley)	1b	1910-2
'Terra Nova'	1B	
Shackleton (with Mawson, Priestley & Wild)	2a	1907-9
Shackleton (with Polar party & Wild)	2A	1908
Mawson (with Western party)	2B	1908
Priestley (with Northern party)	2C	1908
Shackleton (with Wild)	2b	1914-6
Shackleton (on 'James Caird')	2c	1916
Shackleton (with Wild)	2d	1921-2
Wild (after death of Shackleton)	2D	1922
Amundsen	3	1910-2
Mawson (with Wild)		1911-4
'Aurora' (taking expedition south)	4a	1911-2
Mawson (sledging parties with Ninnis & Mertz)	4A	1912-3
Wild (sledging parties)	4B	1912-3
'Aurora' (to relieve expedition)	4b	1912-3
'Aurora' (to pick up Mawson)	4c	1913-4
Mawson (on 'Discovery')	4d	1929-30
Mawson	4e	1930-1

© Geographical Projects

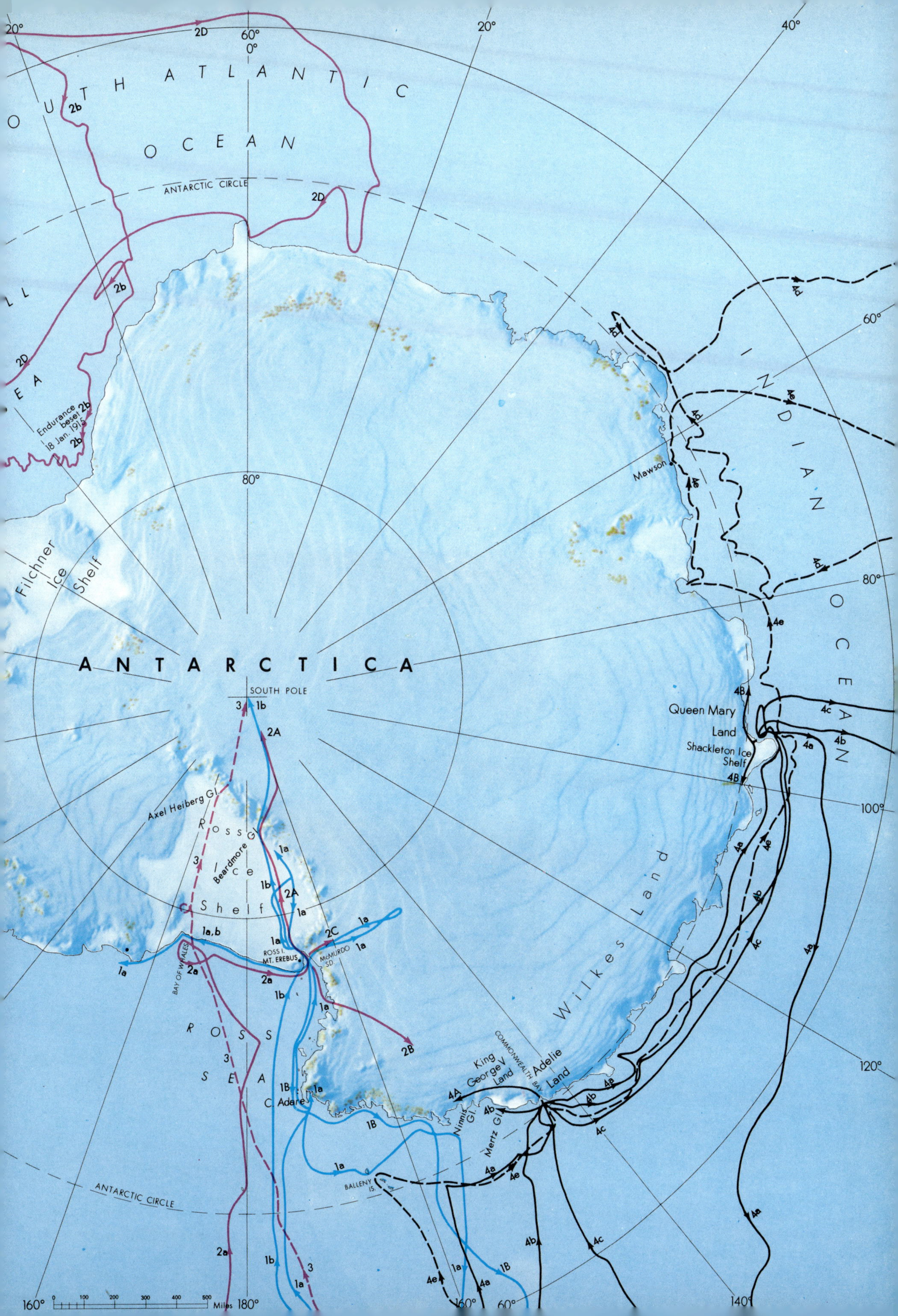

SOUTH ATLANTIC OCEAN

ANTARCTIC CIRCLE

ANTARCTICA

Filchner Ice Shelf

SOUTH POLE

Axel Heiberg Gl.

Beardmore Gl.

ROSS Ice Shelf

ROSS I.
MT. EREBUS
McMURDO SD.

BAY OF WHALES

ROSS SEA

C. Adare

BALLENY IS.

Wilkes Land

Queen Mary Land
Shackleton Ice Shelf

Mawson

INDIAN OCEAN

King George V Land
Commonwealth Bay
Adélie Land
Nimrod Gl.
Mertz Gl.

Endurance beset 18 Jan. 1915

ANTARCTIC CIRCLE

80°

60°

40°

20°

0°

20°

40°

60°

80°

100°

120°

140°

160°

180°

Miles
0 100 200 300 400 500

3 1b
2A
1a
1b
2A
1a
1a,b
1a
2C
1a
2a
2a
1b
1a
2B
1B
1a
1B
2a
1b
3

4A
4b
4a
4c
4a
4b
4a
4c
4a
4b
4c
4e
4a
4e
1a
1B
4e
4a

Above: a photograph taken by Bowers
on the polar plateau, showing the other
four men hauling the sledge. From left
to right they are Evans, Oates, Wilson,
and Scott. By this time they were
weakening, and the task must have been
agonizing. Scott wrote, ''God help us,
we can't keep pulling, that is certain.
Amongst ourselves we are unendingly
cheerful, but what every man feels
in his heart, I can only guess.''

second hour of that march, Bowers' sharp eyes detected what he thought was a cairn. . . . Half an hour later he detected a black speck. . . . We marched on and found that it was a black flag tied to a sledge bearer; nearby the remains of a camp . . . this told us the whole story. The Norwegians have forestalled us and are first at the Pole. It is a terrible disappointment for me and I am very sorry for my loyal companions."

On January 17, 1912, Scott reached the pole, where he found Amundsen's tent and the letter he had left behind, addressed to Scott. The exhausted and discouraged Englishmen built a cairn near Amundsen's tent, unfurled their Union Jack and photographed themselves at the Pole. For Scott who had for years dreamed of being the first to stand at the position of the South Pole, it was a bitter experience. "Great God! this is an awful place. . . ." he wrote. "Now for the run home and a desperate struggle. I wonder if we can do it?"

The next day the return journey began—800 miles across the most difficult terrain in the world. The health of the men began to worry Scott, as scurvy, frostbite, and fatigue became constant complaints. On January 25, he wrote: "Only 89 miles to the next

Below: a drawing by Wilson of one of the sledging party getting ready for a night away from the base. In the foreground the sledge can be seen, half-buried by the gale-swept snow. Scott's party was plagued by blizzards.

depot, but it is time we cleared off this plateau . . . Oates suffers from a very cold foot; Evans' fingers and nose are in a bad state and tonight Wilson is suffering tortures from his eyes . . . I fear a succession of blizzards at this time of year . . . not only stopping our marches but the cold damp air takes it out of us. . . ."

At the same time as Scott wrote these words more than 700 miles deep in the Antarctic solitude, Amundsen was arriving at his base camp near the Bay of Whales. It had taken him 99 days to cover 1,860 miles in his conquest of the pole with an ease that made the feat seem less than it was. Luck had contributed to his success. But his use of dogs rather than ponies, the skill with which he had

Above: the Scott party at the pole, their Union Jack fluttering sadly near the Norwegian flag left by the Amundsen expedition. After all their struggles they arrived at the goal to discover that they were simply the second party to reach the pole, that all their grinding fatigue and hardships had been endured for so poor a prize. This photograph, with the others taken on their journey, was developed from negatives found with their bodies eight months later. Left to Right: Oates, Bowers, Scott, Wilson, Evans. Bowers took the photograph by pulling a string attached to the camera-shutter.

placed his food depots, and his determination were equally responsible. Yet even while he and his companions celebrated their safe
return tragic events were taking place to the south.

On February 7, Scott and his men reached the head of the Beardmore Glacier where naked rock was exposed by the blasting winds.
Even with their disappointment and being completely worn down
by the endless days of cold they managed to maintain sufficient
morale and strength to collect 30 pounds of rocks from the region.
These were to be transported back to the base camp for examina-
tion by the expedition geologist. Then on their way down the
glacier, they became lost and wasted so much time that food rations

Above: Robert Falcon Scott. In this
detail from the photograph opposite
his face shows clearly all his tension
and bitter disappointment.

had to be reduced. By the time the flag marking the next depot had at last been sighted, there was one meal left for each man. While they were descending the glacier, the seaman in the group, Edgar Evans, fell twice and injured his head. He became dazed and incoherent, and as Scott recorded in his journal, "He (Evans) is absolutely changed from his normal self-reliant self." On February 17, when they reached the bottom of the glacier, Evans became unable to keep pace with the other men, and frequently someone had to stay behind with him. Then one day he dropped to his knees

Above: a charcoal drawing by Edward Wilson of three men cramped together in a tiny tent, drawn on a previous expedition with Scott eight years before the tragic South Pole journey. It must have been very similar to the last sad days when Scott, Wilson, and Bowers lay trapped by the storm after Evans and Oates were gone. It was in that tent that the rescue party found them, lying peacefully in death, with Scott's arm thrown protectively over Wilson, his friend.

Right: Captain Oates walking out into the blizzard on his frostbitten feet, going to his death in an attempt to give his comrades the chance to survive.

with his clothing disarranged, his hands uncovered and badly frostbitten, and "a wild look in his eyes." That night Evans lapsed into a coma and died. The others were still 430 torturous miles from their base camp.

The Army officer, Captain Oates, was the next man to weaken. He could no longer pull a sledge, but trudged alongside despite his painfully frostbitten feet. By March 15, when he realized he could go on no longer, he begged the others to leave him behind to die, which they refused to do. The next day when another blizzard kept

Below: the last page from Scott's diary. When he realized they would not survive, he wrote several moving letters, one of them to Wilson's wife. He said, "If this letter reaches you, Bill and I will have gone out together. We are very near it now and I should like you to know how splendid he was at the end—everlastingly cheerful and ready to sacrifice himself for others, never a word of blame to me for leading him into this mess . . . I can do no more to comfort you than to tell you that he died as he lived, a brave, true man—the best of comrades and staunchest of friends. My whole heart goes out to you in pity. Yours, R. Scott."

Below right: Scott's hut near McMurdo Station and beyond it the cross erected in memory of the unlucky expedition. In Britain the whole nation was plunged into mourning—and Scott and his companions became national heroes.

all four inside the tent, Oates made an excuse for going outside for a few minutes. He shuffled out into the blizzard and was never seen again.

Then the cooking and heating fuel that was vital to their survival began to run low. Somehow, it had evaporated from the cans where it was stored. The danger of freezing to death was now added to the threats of frostbite, hunger, and fatigue. Two days after Oates' disappearance Scott wrote: "We have the last half-fill of oil in our primus and a very small quantity of spirit — this alone between us and. . . ."

On March 21, when they were only 11 miles from their last food depot, yet another blizzard blew up and forced them to make camp. Whirling whiteness and cold pinned the three survivors in their tent. They lay there, knowing that only a short distance away lay thousands of pounds of food.

During this awful period of desolation, Scott still had the strength to record his thoughts in the now-famous journal. "Had we lived, I should have had a tale to tell of the hardihood, endurance, and cour-

age of my companions that would have stirred the heart of every Englishman. These rough notes and our dead bodies must tell the tale, but surely, surely, a great rich country like ours will see that those who are dependent on us are properly provided for."

About a week later he made this final entry in the journal: ". . . Every day now we have been ready to start for our depot *eleven miles* away, but outside the door of the tent, it remains a scene of whirling drift. I do not think we can hope for any better things now. We shall stick it out to the end, but we are getting weaker, of course, and the end cannot be far.

"It seems a pity, but I do not think I can write more.

R. Scott.

"For God's sake look after our people."

Eight months passed before their bodies were found. Wilson and Bowers were lying with their sleeping bags closed. Scott's bag was open. One arm was thrown across Wilson, perhaps his closest friend. In a bag lying near the bodies were the 30 pounds of Beardmore rocks the men had carried with them to the end.

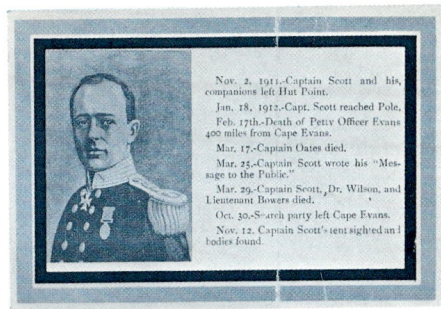

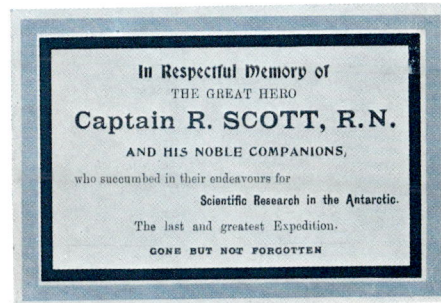

Nov. 2, 1911.-Captain Scott and his companions left Hut Point.
Jan. 18, 1912.-Capt. Scott reached Pole.
Feb. 17th.-Death of Petty Officer Evans 400 miles from Cape Evans.
Mar. 17.-Captain Oates died.
Mar. 25.-Captain Scott wrote his "Message to the Public."
Mar. 29.-Captain Scott, Dr. Wilson, and Lieutenant Bowers died.
Oct. 30.-Search party left Cape Evans.
Nov. 12. Captain Scott's tent sighted and bodies found.

In Respectful Memory of
THE GREAT HERO
Captain R. SCOTT, R.N.
AND HIS NOBLE COMPANIONS,
who succumbed in their endeavours for
Scientific Research in the Antarctic.
The last and greatest Expedition.
GONE BUT NOT FORGOTTEN

Above: In Memoriam cards for Scott.

Right: Douglas Mawson. He was already an experienced Antarctic traveler when in 1911–12 he took the first Australian expedition to the Southern Continent, an expedition not without tragedy.

Below: the interior of an Antarctic building. Unless a building is heated, even the moisture in breath will produce these ice formations hanging from the ceiling—frozen condensation. Mawson named his hut at Commonwealth Bay "The Home of the Blizzard."

The Home of the Blizzard

8

The Antarctic "summer" of 1911–1912 had seen the South Pole conquered twice, with relative ease by Roald Amundsen, tragically by Robert F. Scott. During November and December, 1911, when these two were racing toward the pole, the first Australian expedition to Antarctica was heading for the region between Oates Land and Wilhelm II Land. This was the coastline that had not been visited since the days of Charles Wilkes and Dumont d'Urville and was virgin territory for exploration.

The leader of the Australian group was the English-born Douglas Mawson, an experienced Antarctic traveler and scientist who had climbed Mount Erebus on an earlier expedition. On another journey he had accompanied a Professor T. W. E. David to the South Magnetic Pole. His aim this time was the scientific and geographical exploration of the area between Oates Land and Wilhelm II Land. To make this easier Mawson planned to set up three separate exploring bases on Antarctica that would keep in touch with one another by short-wave radio.

The ship that took the Australians south was an old sealer called the *Aurora*. By January, 1912, it had gone eastward along the Antarctic coast until Mawson saw a suitable site for their main winter base on Cape Denison in Commonwealth Bay.

The area around the camp site was a vast and flat expanse of ice

Below: members of Mawson's expedition gathering ice for water during a blizzard. The power of the icy wind sweeping over the open expanses of the polar continent knocks men off their feet, so that they must almost crawl about when outdoors.

Above: long crevasses in the Antarctic. Here they are visible, with a thin coat of ice over them that is covered with snow. Frequently the snow covering lies even with the surrounding surface, so that the first indication of their presence is that the ice cracks open when a weight travels over the top.

shelf that got steeper toward the south. Because of the unceasing winds that blew throughout the region Mawson nicknamed their Commonwealth Bay camp "The Home of the Blizzard." Once, a wind speed of 63.6 miles per hour was recorded, and occasionally gusts of up to 200 miles per hour were registered at the weather station set up near the camp. There was always a wind—a screaming gale that dominated the lives of Mawson and his companions. The men had to lean so far forward as they walked into the direction of the wind that a sudden lull would make them lunge forward and fall. Without the $1\frac{1}{2}$-inch spikes attached to the soles of their boots, they would have been unable to make any progress at all against the winds. On one occasion, Mawson saw a 3,000-pound tractor tossed 50 yards into the air by a sudden gust. The constant blizzards brought perpetual darkness, unrelieved by the starlight that in calm weather gives Antarctic winters an eery light.

Despite the furious winds and interminable darkness, Mawson stuck to his intention of making systematic scientific observations. The meteorological hut had to be visited regularly so that records of the weather changes could be made. In his journal Mawson des-

cribed a typical trip to the hut of a man crawling on his hands and knees to keep himself from being blown away. Almost immediately as he emerged from the warmth of a camp building, the man's eyebrows and beard would become frozen and covered with tiny icicles. If he stopped for a moment and put his hand six inches in front of his face, the mittened hand would be hidden by the whirling snow that continually filled the air. When he had crawled along for what seemed to be the distance to the hut, the man would reach out and grope for the door of the hut. Once the door had been found, the man would have to cling to it and with a free hand try to open it enough so that he could squeeze into the hut. Often after such a journey over and back to take a look at the instruments, the man would see that a patch of skin on his face, or a finger, had been frostbitten.

After spending 10 months at the Home of the Blizzard the Australians embarked on their explorations, dividing themselves up into five separate parties. For the next few months four of these groups would concentrate on making systematic explorations of the coastal regions and the inland ice sheet of King George V Land.

Above: Mawson staring in horror down the crevasse into which Ninnis had just disappeared with the sledge that carried most of their food. The hole in the snow was 11 feet across, opening above a crack that went deep below them. There was no sign of him. Mawson and Mertz stayed by the hole calling for hours. No one answered. Below: Lieutenant B. E. S. Ninnis.

Mawson had two men in his group and they were to explore the coast from Cape Denison to Oates Land. One of them was an Englishman, Lieutenant B. E. S. Ninnis, the other was Dr. Xavier Mertz, a young Swiss mountaineer and skiing champion. The group took three sledges to carry provisions and these were pulled by 17 huskies.

By the end of November Mawson's group had its first setback when one of the sledges, loaded with half the food, dropped into a crevasse. Fortunately they were able to haul it out and continue on. But a few days later, in the midst of a two-day blizzard they were forced to abandon the damaged sledge and had to transfer the food and supplies to the remaining two. Most of the food was loaded on to Ninnis' sledge, which the strongest dogs pulled.

On December 14, with the sun shining brightly, they decided to make one last dash to reach their "farthest east" point before turning back to explore farther inland. Mertz, who was on skis, led the way. Mawson was in the middle with the light sledge, and Ninnis brought up the rear with his heavily laden sledge. Where crevasses threaten, the iron rule of travel across snow is to put the heaviest load in the rear.

About noon, Mertz raised his ski pole, a prearranged signal telling the others that he was passing over a crevasse. Mawson carefully examined the snow at the spot but found no signs of weakness and sledged on. Suddenly, he looked ahead to see Mertz gazing back past him in horror. "Behind me," Mawson wrote, "Nothing met my eyes but my own sledge tracks running back in the distance. Where was Ninnis and his sledge?"

Behind them, there was nothing but a gaping hole where their companion had been. Far below, a crack penetrated deep into the ice, and they could see a badly injured dog whimpering on an ice shelf about 150 feet down. Another dog lay motionless beside the first. Ninnis and his sledge had completely disappeared. For three hours the two men shouted into the crevasse. But no answer came from the depths below. Hours went by, and the injured dog finally died. At last, knowing that Ninnis could not be alive, Mawson read aloud a short burial service.

Mawson and Mertz were in desperate straits. They had lost most of their own rations, all the food for the dogs, and the tent. Worse still was the fact that they were 300 miles from base with no reserve supplies of food on the trail behind them. Their only hope was to make a dash for home, killing and eating the dogs to supplement the 1½-weeks' food supply that remained.

Throwing all precautions aside, they began their race against time and weather, risking snow bridges across crevasses in a way they would have thought suicidal before. Their dogs became so weak from hunger, cold, and overwork that most of them died. The few who managed to keep going were eventually shot for the stringy meat that still remained on their bones.

Then Mertz began to weaken. Lack of food and the killing strain

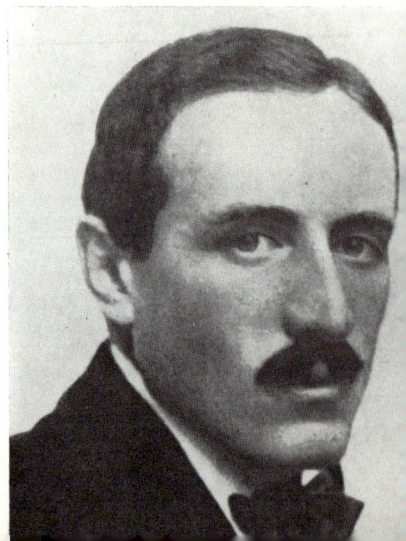

Above: the icecap with its hummocks and ridges. It was over similar very difficult terrain that Mawson had to haul his sledge alone after Mertz died.

Left: Xavier Mertz. He was a young Swiss mountaineer, who was also a skiing champion. When the expedition had divided into four separate groups for exploration, he went with Mawson.

of manhauling the sledge sapped his strength. He was badly frost-bitten but refused to believe it until one day he bit off the end of a finger from which all feeling had gone. By January 1, he could no longer pull the sledge and Mawson had to drag him along on top of it. "Both our chances are going now," wrote Mawson on January 6. The next day Mertz died.

Mawson was alone and still more than 100 miles from the shelter of the Home of the Blizzard. To reduce the weight he had to pull he cut the sledge in half and discarded everything that wasn't essential for survival. By now the skin on his frostbitten feet was beginning to blister, which slowed his pace down to a little more than six miles a day. There seemed little chance that he would ever reach the base camp.

As he was recrossing Mertz Glacier on January 17, Mawson slipped through the snow into a crevasse, dangling on the end of a 14-foot line while the anchoring sledge above inched toward the edge of the crevasse. If it slipped much more, he would be carried to certain death below.

Miraculously the sledge stopped moving. Weakened as he was, Mawson was somehow able to catch hold of a knot in the rope and managed to haul himself up to the rim of the crevasse. But just as he reached the top, the overhanging snow-ledge collapsed. Again, he fell the length of the line.

Somehow Mawson managed to overcome his desperate feelings and the pain of dangling in the rope harness. He climbed up the rope once again, inch by agonizing inch. This time the snow at the top of the crevasse held. He scrambled over the edge and crawled to a safer surface where he lay for an hour, too weak to move. There was very little food left now, but despite his constant hunger Mawson managed to stagger on.

After nearly two more weeks of the most agonising progress he found a cairn that had apparently been left by a search party that had come out from the base camp to look for Mawson, Ninnis, and Mertz. In the cairn Mawson found a bag of food and a note telling him that more supplies had been left 23 miles ahead. The food gave Mawson new strength and he was able to continue his lonely trek to the next food depot, which was only five miles from Commonwealth Bay. As he reached the second cairn, a blizzard struck and prevented him from making any further progress on the five miles between him and the base camp.

Meanwhile, the *Aurora* was being prepared for her return journey to Australia. Even though Mawson had failed to turn up, the captain of the *Aurora* knew that he would have to take the ship on to the Shackleton Ice Shelf to pick up another of the exploring parties that was waiting there. Mawson had told Captain Davis before he had set out with Ninnis and Mertz that Davis should take over command of the expedition if he, Mawson, did not come back. The *Aurora* set sail on February 1, on the very morning that Mawson finally staggered back into the camp at Commonwealth Bay.

Five men were waiting for him there—volunteers who had offered to spend another winter at the Bay in the unlikely hope that Mawson, Ninnis, and Mertz would return. Quickly a message was radioed to the *Aurora* to return. But the ship was unable to get back into the bay because of a hurricane. Furthermore, the party on the Shackleton Ice Shelf, which was led by Frank Wild, an experienced explorer who had been with Robert Scott on an earlier expedition, was unprepared for another winter in the Antarctic. Unless he sailed on, Davis knew that the encroaching winter ice might prevent the *Aurora* from reaching them at all. It was a difficult

decision for Davis to make. Mawson would have to spend another winter in the "Home of the Blizzard," on the continent that had killed his two companions and nearly taken his own life.

Another Antarctic winter descended on Mawson and the men who had stayed behind to wait for him. Again the winds were so strong that they had to crawl across the snow to the meteorological hut to record the temperature and wind speeds. One day in July the instruments in the hut showed an average wind speed of 63.5 miles per hour, and for one eight-hour period it got up to 107 miles per hour. As they had done during the previous winter, the men spent some of their idle hours betting on the average monthly velocity of the wind. The prize was usually a bar of chocolate.

Radio contact with Australia was maintained by sending messages via a small substation on Macquarie Island. It was on this hookup that the men learned of the death of Scott and his men, which had occurred almost exactly a year before. Perhaps Mawson better than anyone else was able to appreciate the isolated desperation and pain of their last hours. To help distract themselves from their own feelings of isolation and boredom the men at the Home of the Blizzard produced their own newspaper called *The Adélie Blizzard*. Much of the news, which was typed out on the typewriter, had been picked up from the radio transmissions they received from Australia. Finally, one day in mid-November, the radio informed them that the

Above: the Mawson expedition that was
in the Antarctic from 1929 to 1931.
Douglas Mawson himself is the third
from the right in the center row. He
recuperated rapidly from his ordeal
and was soon back in the Antarctic.

Aurora had left Australia on its way to pick them up. Several weeks later they saw a faint smudge of smoke on the horizon and knew that the *Aurora* had arrived.

Before they actually set sail for home in mid-December, Mawson asked Captain Davis to take the *Aurora* westward along the coast to the Shackleton Ice Shelf, a glacier-fed platform of ice that extends out into the ocean. This was just another example of Mawson's dedication to science—after an absence of over two years he could still defer his homecoming in order to gain more knowledge about Antarctica. More of the coastline was mapped and more zoological specimens were collected from the ocean. In addition the men on the *Aurora* had a chance to watch the crumbling of a large section of the shelf. As the ship was making its way along the coast about 300 yards out from the cliff, they saw some pieces of ice drop from the top edge of the cliff. Then an enormous slice of the cliff broke off and plunged into the sea with a deep, booming roar. Then it rose again to the surface and began to shed great white masses of itself that pushed toward the ship in an ever-widening field of ice. The main piece of the slice continued to rise high out of the water and then to sink from sight. When this motion ceased the slice had become a beautiful blue iceberg amidst acres and acres of white fragments—the heart of a flower among its fallen petals.

At last in February, 1914, the *Aurora* returned to Australia. Douglas Mawson received worldwide acclaim for his feat. He was still physically broken and it would take years for him to completely recover his strength. But the Antarctic maintained its fascination for Mawson, and he returned for more explorations in 1929.

Below: the *Aurora,* which arrived back at the base camp at Coronation Bay almost a year after Mawson had completed his solitary march.

Above: Vilhjalmur Stefansson, the Canadian explorer who went to the Arctic in 1906 to join the Anglo-American Polar Expedition. Although the expedition never materialized, Stefansson began his lifelong study of the Eskimos. He had an abiding curiosity, an inquiring, original mind, and was to become one of the first scientists to believe in "living off the land"—and to practice his belief.

The Riddle of the Copper Eskimos

9

Charlie Klinkenberg was blessed with boundless energy and fearlessness. As an Arctic sea captain he had few peers. As a ruthless scoundrel he had none. Entrusted with the whaling ship *Olga* by its owner James McKenna, Charlie had one foggy morning in 1905 slipped out of the Yukon port of Herschel without permission and without orders. Steaming eastward, he had looted a storehouse and then sailed farther east to Victoria Island to hunt caribou.

Charlie's adventures might never have been recorded had it not been for the fact that in the spring of 1907 he was to meet with the arctic explorer, Vilhjalmur Stefansson.

In the spring of 1906—a year after Charlie had vanished in the

Above: carved whales' teeth, crafted by a sailor on a whaling ship. The scenes show Eskimo life, hunting bears, reindeer, and seals, traveling in sledges, and living in their igloos.

Arctic fog—this young Canadian explorer had traveled overland from Victoria, British Columbia, then by boat down the Mackenzie River to Herschel Island, which is about 80 miles west of Mackenzie Bay. At Herschel he was to join the Anglo-American Polar Expedition and proceed eastward to Victoria Island aboard the expedition's schooner, the *Duchess of Bedford*. From his book knowledge of the Arctic Stefansson feared that the ship would never reach Herschel Island because it had no auxiliary engines. It was for this reason that he arranged to make his way by rail and river. If the *Duchess of Bedford* failed to get to Mackenzie, Stefansson knew he could spend his time living with the Eskimos of Mackenzie Bay. For a long time

Above: a photograph that Stefansson took of the Mackenzie River Eskimos with whom he lived in the winter of 1906–1907. They were of the Koukga-muit tribe, from the east mouth of the Mackenzie River. By the end of the winter Stefansson had mastered the fundamentals of their language and felt at home in their settlements.

he had been interested in Eskimo life and culture, of which very little was known and even less documented. And he had eagerly accepted an invitation to join the expedition as its anthropologist.

When Stefansson got to Herschel in August there was no sign of the schooner, which of course, did not surprise him. Even though he had always doubted that the ship would come to pick him up, Stefansson had entrusted his entire Arctic outfit to it. If he was going to live with the Eskimos he wanted to do so as one of them— in their houses, dressing like them, and eating what they ate. Thus in August he found himself, in accord with his own plan, set down 200 miles north of the Arctic Circle, with a summer weight suit of clothing, a camera, some notebooks, a rifle, and ammunition. He was facing an Arctic winter, where his only shelter would have to be the roof of some hospitable Eskimo house.

These were ideal conditions for Stefansson who knew that if he had been with an expedition and had lived with the other men in it, he would have lived near the Eskimos, instead of with them. "I should have seen them as an outsider, a stranger. If I had visited

Above: Stefansson was not the first to find the Eskimo pattern of life particularly interesting. This is a drawing by Sir John Ross of an Eskimo village known as North Hendon, near Felix Harbor on the Boothia Peninsula.

them now and then I should have found them wearing their company manners and should have obtained no better insight into their lives than does the ordinary missionary or trader. My very poverty was my greatest advantage; I was not rich and powerful like the whaling captains or mounted policemen, so there was no reason why they should flatter me or show me deference."

The Mackenzie Eskimos of Herschel Island took Stefansson into their houses and treated him hospitably and courteously and exactly as if he were one of them. They gave him clothes to wear and shared their food with him. He in turn helped them with their fishing and hunting and joined in their games until they gradually forgot that he was not one of them. They began to live their lives in front of Stefansson as though he was not there at all.

What Stefansson learned during that winter from October 1906 to March 1907, was to provide him with the incentive to stay five years in the Arctic in order to know more about the Eskimos. Although their language is extremely difficult to learn, by the end of the winter he felt that he had mastered the fundamentals and was able to live among these people without any feeling of isolation.

One day in the spring of 1907 word spread through Herschel that a ship had been sighted. Stefansson thought it might be the *Duchess of Bedford* after all, but when the vessel appeared on the horizon it was seen to be coming from the northeast. The *Duchess* surely would have approached from the west. As the ship approached the harbor on Herschel Island, Stefansson saw the name *Olga* on its bow. The schooner was commanded by Captain Charles Klinkenberg, who met Stefansson when he came ashore.

As the two men talked during the next few days, Klinkenberg had news that particularly interested Stefansson—the *Olga* had wintered on Banks Island to the east of Herschel. Here, Klinkenberg and the men on board had seen Eskimos who were armed with bows and arrows and who used copper tools and who evidently had been in no contact with white men in recent years.

What intrigued Stefansson was the idea that there might really exist on Banks Island and Victoria Island and even on the north shore of the continent of America, Eskimos who had never seen a white man. Perhaps these Eskimos were descendants of men from the Franklin mission or from the many search parties that had gone looking for the lost Englishmen. Stefansson wanted to find out whether human beings really did exist in these remote areas, which were marked with the words "uninhabited" on a map issued by the Canadian government in 1906.

Early in the winter of 1907, Stefansson returned to Canada where he began making plans to go back to the Arctic as soon as possible. (Charlie apparently continued to command the *Olga,* doing some whale hunting to earn money and having an adventurous time.) It was on his return to Canada that Stefansson learned of the fate of the *Duchess of Bedford.* The ice at Point Barrow blocked its farther advance until the beginning of winter and then it had been completely stopped by the floes on the north coast of Alaska at Flaxman Island. The Anglo-American Polar Expedition was now sad history.

Stefansson's keenness to return to the Arctic must have won over the directors of the American Museum of Natural History. They agreed to supply enough money for him to carry out his study of the Eskimos. Then by chance a zoologist and friend of Stefansson's, who was eager to study the birds and animals of the Arctic, was invited to accompany him. This was Dr. Rudolph Martin Anderson.

Right: watercolors of an Eskimo couple, by John White and dated about 1570. The woman (left) is carrying a baby in her hood. Stefansson, exploring the Arctic more than 300 years later, was fascinated by the clothing worn by the Eskimos, which is generally loose-fitting to allow a layer of warm air between clothing and skin.

Right: Eskimos fishing through holes they have made in the ice. Stefansson learned to fish and hunt in the way the Eskimos did, and was very soon able to live in barren surroundings where white men were usually doomed.

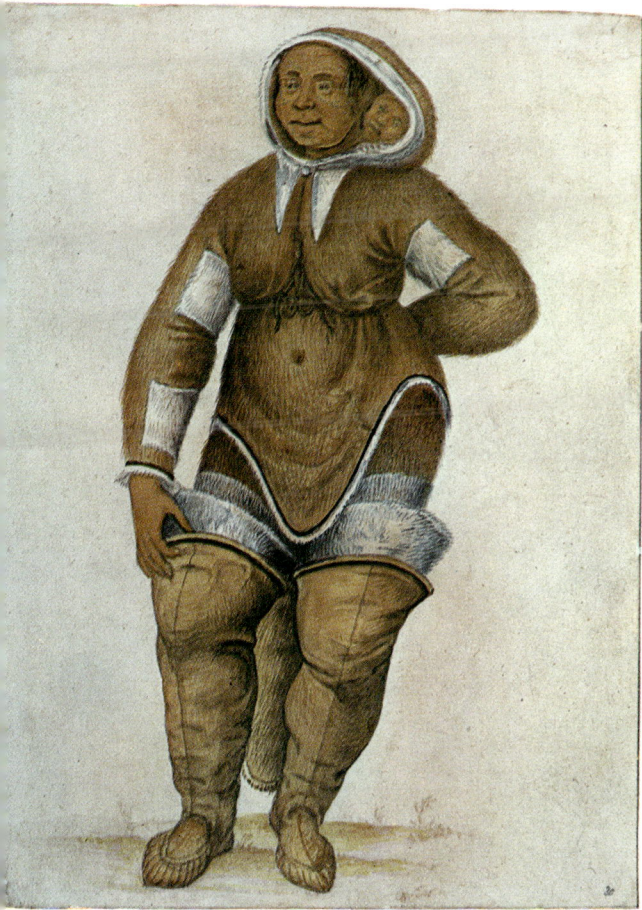

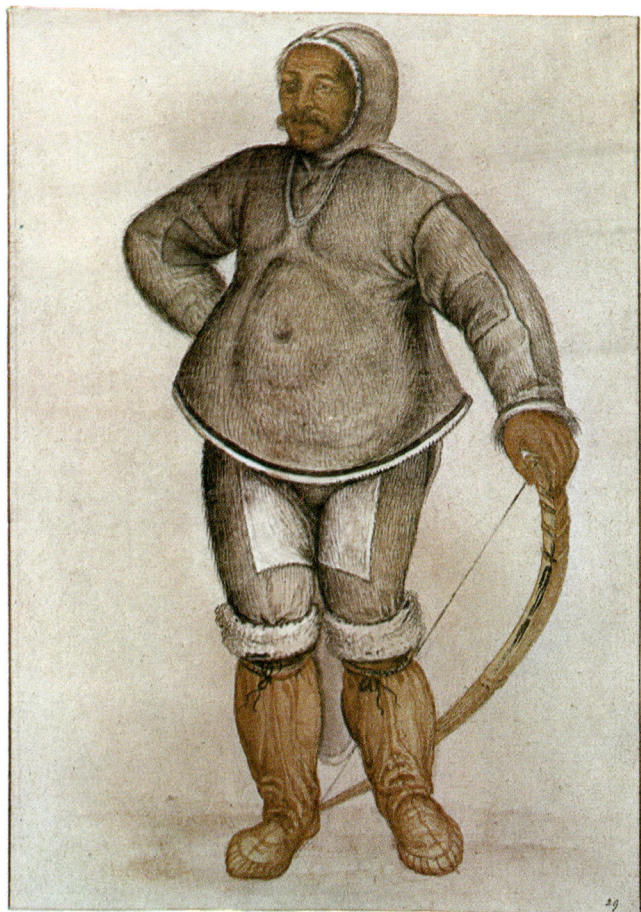

Above: an igloo under construction. Stefansson wrote that the Eskimos illuminated their igloos with lamps burning oil. He said the lamps "were set low down in Eskimo fashion but their light was reflected again and again from the million snow crystals in the dome, so that the house was filled with a soft and diffused glow."

In May, 1908, Stefansson and Anderson headed for the Yukon. Their plan was to get to Herschel, pick up some supplies there, and hitch a ride on a whaler for Victoria Island. As before, Stefansson's equipment was of the simplest kind. He and Dr. Anderson each had a camera and supplies of film, a pair of rifles and plenty of ammunition. They also carried half a dozen rifles and shotguns for the Eskimos to use and a small supply of tobacco that they would give to prospective Eskimo employees. They each had a silk tent, writing materials, and a pair of field glasses, and a couple of cooking utensils —all the essentials for Arctic exploration, except for matches.

By mid-August the two men and the Eskimos they had engaged as guides were at Herschel Island where they expected to be able to buy matches from the whaling ships that stop at the island. At Herschel they also planned to join up with any one of the whalers that they expected would be going east to Victoria Island. But only

one whaler arrived, and it had no extra supplies of matches to sell.

Stefansson then went to the Northwest Mounted Police and explained his predicament, asking them to give, lend, or sell him enough matches to last through the winter. This the commanding officer of the police refused to do. He was certain no white men could survive a winter on Victoria Island and he knew that no one would go there without matches. So to "protect" the explorers the police denied them the one absolutely essential item for such a trip. The officer did nevertheless offer to put up the two men for the winter at Herschel. Stefansson's response was typical, "Since we had not come north to study the habits of the police at Herschel, we decided . . . to head for Point Barrow," where matches and supplies might be had.

The explorers had much the same luck at Point Barrow, where they decided to wait out the winter. But the time was not spent in idleness. Stefansson became friendly with Natkusiak, an Eskimo "who turned out to be the best traveling companion I have ever had of any race." Natkusiak was also fluent in many Eskimo dialects and taught these to Stefansson, who picked them up eagerly and quickly. In the meantime, Anderson made frequent side trips into the mountains to collect zoological specimens.

It was not until August, 1909, that Stefansson, Anderson, and Natkusiak left Point Barrow for Herschel. But almost a year was to pass before Stefansson, Natkusiak, and another Eskimo named Tannaumirk went even farther east into the region south of Victoria Island.

Stefansson's goal was still to find the Eskimos he had heard about from Klinkenberg. On April 21, 1910, the party set out along a stretch of mainland coast thought to be uninhabited. (Anderson, who had weathered a bout of pneumonia during the winter, had returned to the Mackenzie delta to continue his work there.)

About eight days out, after rounding Cape Parry, they came upon the remains of an Eskimo village. The place appeared to have been

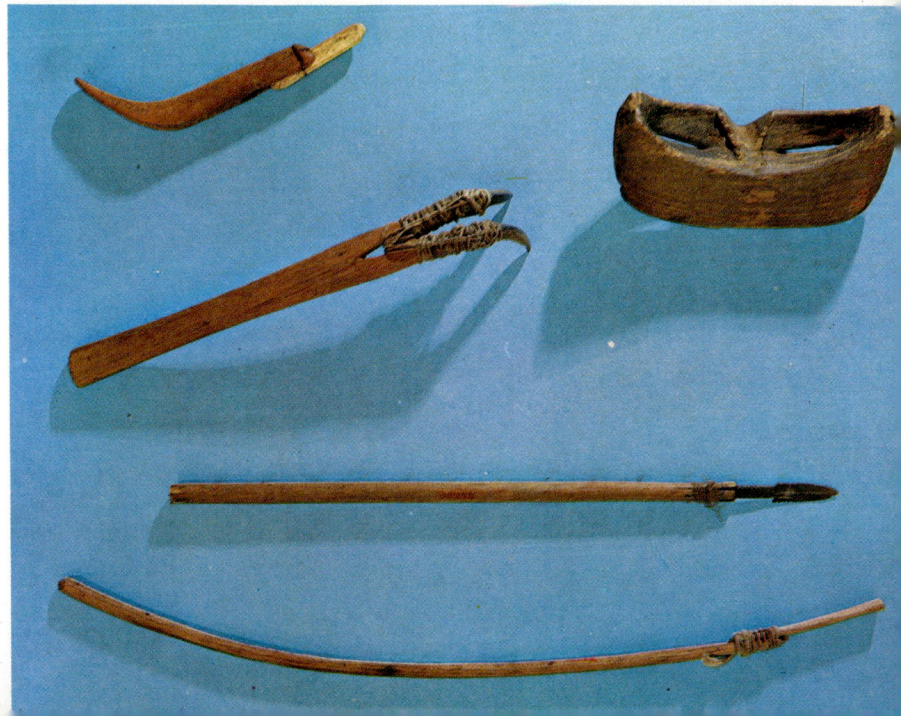

Right: Eskimo hunting equipment that Stefansson collected in the Mackenzie Bay area. Among the implements is a pair of wooden snow goggles, which were worn to prevent snow blindness.

abandoned for a long while, which convinced Natkusiak and Tannaumirk that the region was indeed uninhabited. Stefansson was less certain.

On May 9, they reached Point Wise, where the sea begins to be squeezed between the mainland and the southern shore of Victoria Island. While walking along Stefansson caught sight of a piece of driftwood that seemed to have been hacked by a man-made tool. The next day they saw footprints and sledge tracks. Then during the morning of May 13, they came to a deserted village. Stefansson climbed up on the roof of one of the snow houses to survey the surrounding area. In the distance he saw several men sitting beside some seal holes waiting to spear their prey. After they had driven the sledges nearer to the place where the Eskimo hunters were, Tannaumirk slowly approached them. Suddenly, one of the seal hunters jumped up, holding a long metal knife in his hand. Tannaumirk was quick to explain that he and his companions were friendly. After a while, to convince himself that Tannaumirk was not some sort of evil spirit, the man squeezed Tannaumirk's arm to make sure that he was in fact human. He and the other hunters then invited Tannaumirk, Stefansson, and Natkusiak to come and visit their village.

When they walked into the village, men, women, and children came rushing toward them. After everyone had been introduced, the women hurried off to their houses to cook dinner for their visitors. Then the men got their snow knives and house-building mittens and set about erecting igloos for Stefansson and his two companions.

As he watched and listened Stefansson was hardly able to believe that he was actually seeing not the remains of an ancient civilization but the Stone Age itself. "These people who had never seen a white man until they saw me were completely human men and women, entirely friendly who welcomed us to their homes and bade us stay."

When the snow-house was finished, the Eskimos furnished it with a seal-oil lamp that could be used for cooking and would also provide some warmth to the igloo. Inside they also fashioned a sleeping platform over which were spread reindeer, bear, and musk-ox skins. As the Eskimo men put their final touches to this cozy and comfortable little camp, they told the visitors that their stay in the village was to be a holiday when no hunting would be done.

Right: Vilhjalmur Stefansson in his Eskimo clothing, wearing snow shoes to enable him to move easily across the deep Arctic snows. Throughout his travels from one Eskimo village to another, Stefansson was impressed with the unself-conscious friendliness and the generosity of the people.

Above: while Stefansson was staying with the Mackenzie Bay Eskimos they gave him clothes to wear and taught him how to make his own. This shows the jacket and the hood that he wore.

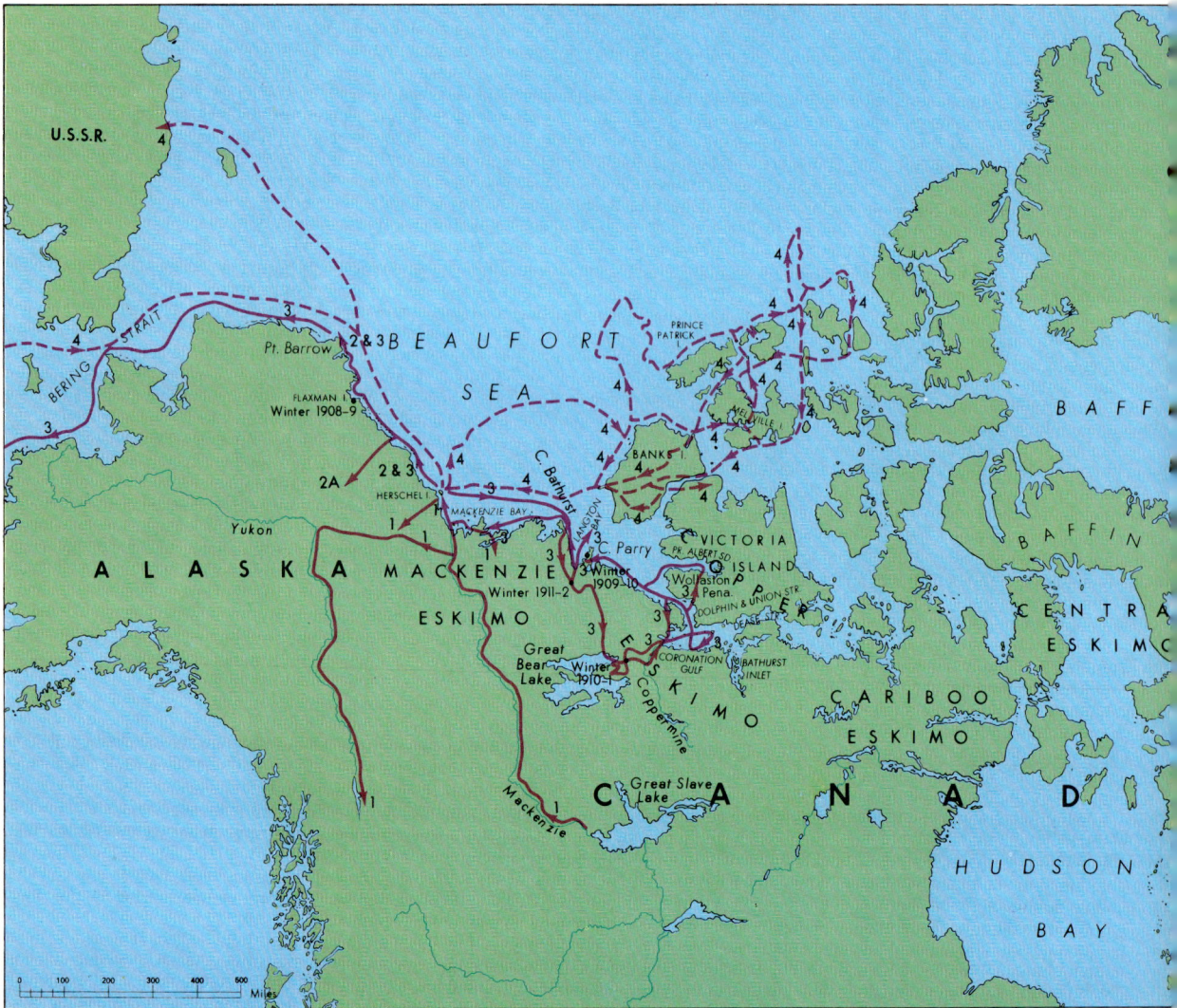

Below: Northern Canada, showing the routes of the Canadian explorer and anthropologist Vilhjalmur Stefansson in the early 1900's.

Stefansson	1	1906–7
Stefansson (with Anderson)	2	1908–9
Anderson	2A	1908–9
Stefansson (with Natkusjak)	3	1910–2
Stefansson	4	1913–8

© Geographical Projects

This was the first time that they had been visited by people from so great a distance and they wanted to have time to learn about the country from which they had come.

That evening after supper Stefansson showed the Dolphin and Union Straits people how to light a sulfur match and the next day the even greater marvel of his rifle. The language they spoke was very similar to that which he had learned from the Mackenzie River Eskimos, and from the start they were all able to understand one another.

During the next few days as he rested and ate and talked with the Dolphin and Union Straits Eskimos Stefansson tried to find out as much as possible about their customs and beliefs. One of the things that interested him most was their acceptance of his appearance—especially his blue eyes and light brown beard. These were characteristics very unlike the Eskimos' dark eyes and straight black hair. But they told him their neighbors to the north had eyes and beards exactly like his—if he wished they would take him the next day to visit their friends on Victoria Island.

After a journey of 16 miles Stefansson, Tannaumirk, and Natkusjak accompanied by one of the men from the Dolphin and Union tribe came upon another village. Here half of the Haneragmiut people of Victoria Island were camped. Although everyone was asleep, they soon came out of their houses and gathered around Stefansson's guide. There were a few moments of excited questioning, while the Haneragmiuts made sure that they were friendly visitors. Then after some rather formal introductions, Stefansson was again treated to the same unaffected kindliness, the same hospitality and good manners he had become used to in the previous camp. The Haneragmiuts fed their visitors the usual Eskimo dinner of boiled meat and fatty soup with seal or caribou blood in it. Afterward they were invited to sleep in the igloos that had been quickly built for their stay.

For more than a year Vilhjalmur Stefansson lived in the region of the Victoria Island people and their neighbors to the south who had villages near the Coronation Gulf. During this time he had an opportunity to observe very closely their physical characteristics, which suggested that they were of mixed Eskimo and white blood. These people were later to be referred to as the "blond Eskimos," but to Stefansson, who was a trained anthropologist, they were only blond in the sense that the men who did have beards had light-brown ones. (Many Eskimos pulled out their beards by the roots as the North Americans did.) The hair on their heads was a dark, rusty brown color and only ten out of a thousand "blond Eskimos" he saw had blue eyes. It was the proportions of the body and the shape of their heads that led Stefansson to suggest that the people of this region were descended from the Viking colonists of Greenland. In the 1400's, when the Greenlanders seem to have died out, one of two things could have happened. The surviving Norsemen may have intermarried with the Eskimos in Greenland. More probably,

Above: an Eskimo spearing a fish. The Copper Eskimos that Stefansson found lived entirely by fishing and hunting. Many of the white men who died in the Arctic wilderness—such as the men of Sir John Franklin's expedition—might have survived the hostile conditions if they had learned to fish and hunt from the Eskimos they encountered.

according to Stefansson, they may have migrated westward to North America where they settled down with the people they found there.

What interested Stefansson most about the people in the region of Victoria Island—or the Copper Eskimos as he called them—was their way of life. He was continually impressed by their friendliness and by the way in which they had obviously managed to survive the hardships of the Arctic. These people who made for themselves simple copper tools and hunting implements, lived a useful existence relying entirely on their luck at hunting and fishing to keep themselves alive. Their self-reliance made Stefansson think of the needless starving of the Franklin mission. "At the very time when these Englishmen were dying of hunger, there were living about them Eskimo families who were taking care of their aged and bringing up their children, unaided by the rifles and other excellent implements which the Englishmen had in abundance."

Exactly a year after his first discovery of the Copper Eskimos on Victoria Island, Stefansson and Natkusiak took their sledges across the island and crossed the Wollaston Peninsula. They were heading for Prince Albert Sound, where they had been told many tribes of Copper Eskimos gathered in the spring for a trading

festival. As they got near the Sound, Stefansson climbed to a high spot of ground. With his binoculars he could see a native village on the ice approximately in the middle of Prince Albert Sound. Stefansson and Natkusiak turned their sledges in the direction of the village which, as they got closer, seemed to be the largest village they had yet come upon. When they arrived Stefansson noted that a greater percentage of these Eskimos looked like Europeans than he had found elsewhere. They were also the most prosperous of the Copper Eskimos. What seemed most remarkable was the extent of their yearly migrations. They had a much greater knowledge of their own country and of others. They also remembered hearing stories from their parents about large sailing ships that had roamed the waters to the east of Victoria Island during the years of the search for Franklin's mission.

In May, 1912, Stefansson and Natkusiak began going westward away from Victoria Island. At Langton Bay they met up again with Dr. Anderson, who with his small party of Eskimos had been continuing his zoological studies. Because Stefansson wanted to visit every Eskimo village along the coast between Langton Bay and Point Barrow, Alaska, he decided not to return with Dr. Anderson to the United States immediately, but to take Natkusiak

Above: seal hunting in Baffin Bay around 1800. Europeans hunted seals in groups like this, but Stefansson found that Eskimos usually hunted alone. Different tribes hunted in different fashions. The Mackenzie Bay people crawled up pretending to be a seal, and then captured their prey by surprise. The Victoria Island men would sit at seal holes for hours, waiting for the seal to come out. Below: an Eskimo mask for dancing.

Above- an Eskimo calendar. Each hole represents a day. The seven holes at the front represent one week. The upper 12 rows of holes are days arranged into the months of the year.

with him and make their way slowly up the coast by sledge.

In a sense the results of Vilhjalmur Stefansson's Arctic travels and his meeting the Copper Eskimos were too spectacular. By the time he returned to the United States (via Point Barrow and by boat through the Bering Sea) there was already some controversy about his explorations. A Seattle, Washington, newspaper had heard about the Copper Eskimos and Stefansson's speculations about their origins. One of the paper's reporters wrote an article claiming that they were "a lost tribe of 1,000 white people, who are believed to be direct descendants from the followers of Leif Erikson who came to Greenland from Iceland about the year 100 and a few years later discovered the north coast of America." This story was supposedly based on an interview with Stefansson.

But as we know, Stefansson had merely suggested various theories for the origin of the Eskimos he found on Victoria Island. The story was out—true or not. And Stefansson was consequently criticized by other anthropologists, some of whom doubted that he had actually discovered the Copper Eskimos. Stefansson was hurt by their doubts and accusations—he had never claimed himself the discoverer of these people. Charlie Klinkenberg and the crew of the *Olga* had first seen these Eskimos during the winter of 1906 when they had wintered near Banks Island.

Even though the controversy over the Copper Eskimos would perhaps never be settled, Stefansson was able to produce various copper tools and items of clothing that the Copper Eskimos had given him. There was also the evidence provided by Dr. John Rae who, a half century earlier, had seen "blond Eskimos" who came from the southwest corner of Victoria Island. Sir John Franklin in an 1824 voyage had noticed "blond traits" among the Eskimos he encountered. Even as long ago as 1585 John Davis had referred to blond Eskimos living on Greenland.

For Stefansson, the Copper Eskimo controversy soon became a waste of time. There were more Eskimos to be studied and more regions of the Arctic to be explored. The Arctic should become the servant of man—not his conquerer. Moreover, the identity of its native people should be preserved. These were the principles to which Stefansson dedicated the remaining 50 years of his life, and the principles that guided him as he returned to the Arctic again and again.

Three veterans of the Arctic: Vilhjalmur Stefansson in the center flanked by Robert Peary and Adolphus Greeley, who had also tried to reach the North Pole. In spite of criticism received from some anthropologists, Stefansson had a very distinguished career. In 1947, he became the Arctic consultant to Dartmouth College, where he remained until his death in 1962. Among the students he trained was Hubert Wilkins, an Australian who tried in 1931 to reach the North Pole in a submarine.

Shackleton in the Antartic

10

While Douglas Mawson was inching his way across the ice of George V Land another polar veteran was dreaming of the most ambitious expedition ever launched in Antarctica. An Irishman named Ernest Shackleton planned to cross the South Pole and complete the first transcontinental journey from the Weddell Sea to the Ross Sea. His scheme involved the cooperation of two separate groups of men. While one group braved the Weddell Sea to land on the newly discovered Filchner Ice Shelf, the second one would land on the Ross Ice Shelf and lay a trail of supply depots up the Beardmore Glacier. These depots would be used by Shackleton and five men

The handwritten sketch map shows the Antarctic Continent with labels including S. AFRICA, WEDDELL SEA, ANTARCTIC Continent, MAGNETIC Pole, S. Pole, ROSS SEA, DEPARTURE, BASE, N.Z., S. AMERICA, and various calculations.

Above: Ernest Shackleton. He was 40 when he decided on his ambitious plan for exploration in Antarctica. He had joined the merchant navy when he was 16, and had gained wide experience at sea. He was said to be a gambler in spirit, always ready to take a chance.

Left: a sketch map that Shackleton drew on a menu for his neighbor at a dinner party to show the route he proposed for crossing the Antarctic continent via the South Pole. He was planning to start from the Weddell Sea and end at the Ross Sea, crossing Antarctica at its narrowest point.

in the last stages of the continental crossing, as they descended the glacier from the South Pole.

The Imperial Trans-Antarctic Expedition, as it was called, had a budget of about $250,000—much of this sum having been contributed by a Scottish industrialist named Sir James Caird. Two ships were purchased for the expedition—the ancient *Aurora* that had been used by Mawson, and a specially constructed vessel that was named *Endurance,* after Shackleton's family motto. The *Aurora,* which was prepared for the expedition in Australia, was to sail from Tasmania to take the Ross Sea party to their allotted task.

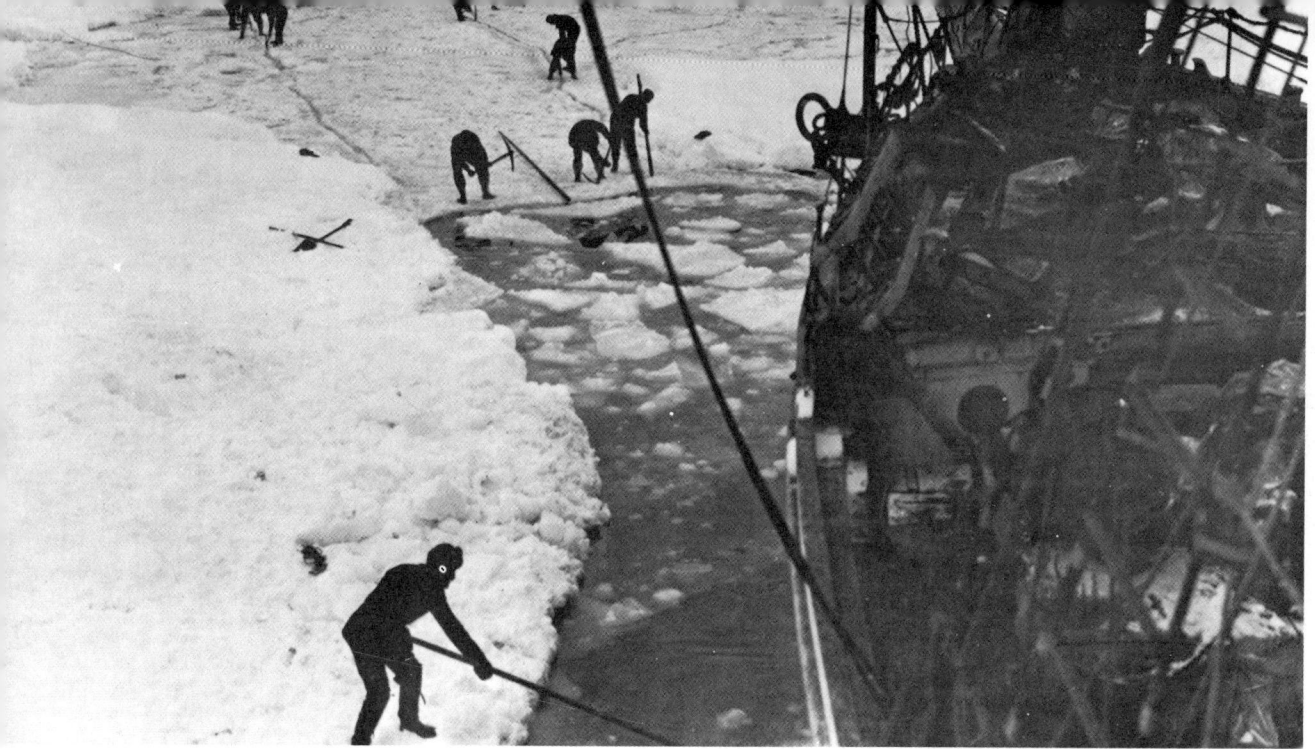

Above: crew members of the *Endurance* trying to cut through the ice to a lead ahead in February, 1915. The pack ice in the Weddell Sea moves in a clockwise direction, due to the prevailing winds and water currents and the geography of the sea. The ship was caught in the drift and moved away from her destination. As she drifted the pressure increased. Shackleton wrote, "The effects of the pressure around were awe-inspiring. If the ship was once gripped firmly, her fate would be sealed!"

The *Endurance* set sail from London on August 8, 1914—just four days after the beginning of World War I when England declared war on Germany. Before leaving Shackleton had offered to put his ship and men at the service of the British government. Mr. Winston Churchill, then First Lord of the Admiralty, had thanked him for the offer but instructed Shackleton to proceed with the expedition.

In December, the *Endurance* left South Georgia Island, despite reports from whaling ships of exceptionally bad ice conditions in the Weddell Sea. Only two days out from South Georgia Island the *Endurance* began to run into heavy ice. It became thicker and by January 19, 1915, the pack closed around the ship. It was a helpless prisoner. Two weeks later, a lead of open water appeared near the ship, and the men tried frantically to free the *Endurance*. But the ice refroze as fast as the men could hack their way through it. By mid-February when they were only 60 miles from the Filchner Ice Shelf the *Endurance* became the expedition's official winter station.

It was frozen into a great slab of pack ice almost three miles square that was drifting slowly to the northwest. Three months went by, enlivened only by dog races on the ice and a narrow escape by one of the men from killer whales. Then, around the middle of May, ice floes began to jostle the ship. The ice that had held the *Endurance* in its grip like a giant vise now began to squeeze it. Another two months went by and finally, on August 1, the floe in which they were embedded cracked in two. The border of ice that

had protected the *Endurance* for so long was now gone. It was exposed to the full pressure of the ice pack, and destruction seemed inevitable.

At the end of October, after having spent 10 months entrapped by ice, Shackleton ordered that all the boats, sledges, and provisions should be moved off the ship. The next day, the *Endurance* had to be abandoned. A pressure ridge that moved across the pack heaved the ship to the top of the ice like a toy. "At last," Shackleton wrote, "the twisting, grinding floes were working their will on the ship. It was a sickening sensation to feel the decks breaking up under one's feet, the great beams bending and then snapping with a noise like heavy gunfire. . . . The floes, with the force of millions of tons of moving ice behind them, were simply annihilating the ship."

Shackleton and his men were now castaways on the treacherous ice 573 miles from the point where the *Endurance* was first beset in February. The nearest land where they might find shelter was Paulet Island, 346 miles away. So, on December 23, they set out. Unfortunately a rise in temperature softened the ice and made the going difficult. After 7 days of toil, they found they had gone only 7½

Above: a banjo, the last thing to be saved from the *Endurance* as she was crushed by the ice. They took it all the way to the Elephant Island camp. Below: the *Endurance*, caught by the pressure of the ice, heeling over.

miles in a straight line—the drift of the pack was against them.

At their present rate of speed, Shackleton calculated that it would take almost 18 months for them to reach safety—if the ice did not disappear under them during the summer thaw. They had enough food to last for only 1½ months.

Shackleton knew that it was hopeless to go on and decided that they should camp on the ice floe. This was appropriately named Patience Camp and here they lived for 3½ months, occasionally shooting penguins and seals for food when their supplies ran out. They narrowly escaped death when two enormous icebergs moved down through the pack like a pair of scissors, missing the camp by only a few yards. Another day, a fanged leopard seal charged into camp in pursuit of one of the men. The seal was shot to death by Frank Wild —the explorer who had accompanied Mawson to the Antarctic and was now on his fourth trip to the frozen continent.

Early in April, the pack began to break up and the leads of open water became larger. Shackleton decided to make for Deception Island, where they could find some food and where whaling ships occasionally stopped. Loading their supplies into the boats, the men set off through the shifting floes toward the north. The first night they camped on an ice floe that split in two beneath one of the tents. Shackleton pulled one of the men, still in his sleeping bag, out of the water seconds before the edges of the floe crashed together again with sickening force. Later the same night, Shackleton found himself drifting away from the main floe on a small cake of ice. A boat had to be sent through the darkness to bring him back.

In mid-April, 1916, the wind shifted and Shackleton decided to try to get to Elephant Island, 100 miles away. In their haste to leave they forgot to bring along a supply of ice for making water and until they were able to collect some "land" ice the men suffered from thirst. For days they rowed and sailed through a maze of drifting and colliding icebergs until they finally got to Elephant Island. It was a barren and inhospitable place. No one would think of searching for them there. The nearest manned station was at South Georgia Island, 870 miles away across the stormiest seas in the world. Yet someone had to make the desperate attempt to reach it.

Shackleton picked five men to accompany him on the risky voyage, leaving the rest of the men on Elephant Island under the command of Frank Wild. Their boat, the *James Caird,* was an undecked lifeboat from the *Endurance,* only 23 feet long and 6 feet wide. The expedition's carpenter built a crude decking of canvas for it that was battened down with sledge runners, but this was fragile protection against the storms that lay ahead.

On April 24, 1916—almost two years after leaving England—the six men set off on their desperate search for help. Gale after gale raged over them. The salt spray froze as it touched the boat rigging, threatening to tip the craft over with its weight. The men inched their way across the slippery deck to chip away at the ice while waves 50 feet high and 100 yards from crest to crest rolled beneath

Right: the crew members after their landing on Elephant Island, having their first drink and hot food for three days. As Elephant Island is only a large chunk of rock with barren, glacier-capped peaks and cliffs, it took them hours to find a small strip of beach to land on and make their camp. Even then, it was not sheltered enough, and their tents were ripped to shreds by the wind soon after they had been put up. The men spent the rest of their stay in one of the upturned boats.

Right: Shackleton might have remembered his old camps as places of comparative luxury compared to the bleak beach of Elephant Island. The hut he set up in 1907–09 can be seen here covered with snow. One of the dog kennels is still visible in the foreground.

them. Many times it appeared as though the *James Caird* would sink.

On the 11th day out, it seemed that all their agonies were in vain. Shackleton later described the scene in his book *South:* "At midnight I was at the tiller and suddenly noticed a line of clear sky between the south and southwest. I called to the men that the sky was clearing, and then, a moment later, I realized that what I had seen was not a rift in the clouds but the white crest of an enormous wave. During twenty-six years' experience of the ocean in all its moods, I have never seen a wave so gigantic. It was a mighty upheaval of the ocean, a thing quite apart from the big white-capped seas that had been our tireless enemies for many days. I shouted 'For God's Sake, hold on! It's got us!' Then came a moment of suspense that seemed drawn out into hours. . . . We felt our boat lifted and flung forward like a cork in a breaking surf. We were in a seething chaos of tortured water; but somehow the boat lived through it, half full of water, sagging to the dead weight and shuddering under the blow. We bailed with the energy of men fighting for life, flinging the water over with every receptacle that came into our hands; and after ten minutes of uncertainty we felt the boat renew her life beneath us. She floated again and ceased to lurch drunkenly as though dazed by the attack of the sea."

Shackleton and his companions were still to endure the nightmare of thirst when their supply of water got low. "Our mouths were dry and our tongues swollen." Then on May 9, they saw two birds sitting on a mass of floating seaweed. At noontime two days later they sighted the coast of South Georgia—just 14 days after their departure from Elephant Island. A fresh-water stream flowed down to the beach where later that day they landed. As the men climbed stiffly out of the boat they then dropped quickly on their knees to gulp down icy water. It was a wonderful moment.

Their ordeal was still not over, for the *James Caird* had landed on the south side of the island—150 sea miles away from the whaling station on the northern shore. Shackleton knew that neither the *James Caird* nor his men were likely to survive another ocean voyage, and he decided that he and two of them would have to walk across the unexplored island to seek help.

On May 19, they set out, taking with them a compass, a chronometer, a stove, provisions for three days, a tent, and 50 feet of rope. They began this last incredible journey with only the vaguest idea of where the whaling station was located.

During the first day fog shrouded the glacier they had to climb, lifting enough to reveal a vast crevasse only a few feet away. Again and again they scaled ice-covered ridges only to find their way barred by chasms or steep cliffs. Before nightfall they had somehow to reach lower ground where they could put up a tent. A fog-covered cliff lay below them.

There was only one thing to do—trust themselves to the icy slope. They coiled the ropes into three pads, sat down on the pads, and each man locked his legs around the man in front of him. Shackleton

Right: the tiny whaling station on South Goergia Island that Shackleton and his two companions finally reached after their grueling march across the frozen island, climbing the mountains in the photograph on the way.

Below: an Antarctic ice cave, painted by E. L. Greenfield. It was this sort of beautiful but forbidding landscape that lay all around the marooned men, and through which Shackleton made his incredible 1000 mile journey.

Above: the men of Elephant Island when they were rescued. All had survived, although one man had to have his toes amputated because of frostbite. One of them, writing of the rescue, said, "There, just rounding the island . . . we saw a little ship flying the Chilean flag. We tried to cheer, but excitement had gripped our vocal cords . . . Suddenly she stopped, a boat was lowered, and we could recognize Sir Ernest's figure as he climbed down the ladder. Simultaneously we burst into a cheer, and then one said to the other, 'Thank God, the Boss is safe."

was in the lead and pushed off into the unknown. "We seemed to shoot into space. For a moment my hair fairly stood on end. Then quite suddenly I felt a glow and knew I was grinning. I was actually enjoying it. It was most exhilarating. We were shooting down the side of an almost precipitous mountain at nearly a mile a minute. I yelled with excitement and found that the others were yelling too. It seemed ridiculously safe. To hell with the rocks!" Their "toboggan" stopped safely in a soft snowbank.

Now only one more obstacle stood between them and the whaling station. As they made their way through a narrow gorge at the bottom of the mountain they heard the splash of a water fall. As Shackleton was later to explain, they were at the wrong end of the rushing water. Peering down, they saw a drop of 25 to 30 feet with impassable ice cliffs on both sides. Using the same ropes that had brought them down the mountain, they looped one end of each rope securely over a boulder. Then each man swung off on the free end of his rope, through the waterfall. They emerged at the bottom, cold and wet but unhurt.

When Shackleton and his two companions finally staggered into the whaling station, the men who greeted them were astounded. The story of their 1,000 mile journey seemed too incredible to be true.

Left: the grave of Ernest Shackleton, just a few miles from the point where he landed on South Georgia Island after his epic voyage from Elephant Island.

Immediately a relief party was organized to sail around to the other side of the island to pick up the three men who had stayed behind with the *James Caird*.

The marooned men on Elephant Island were not so lucky. Three rescue efforts were to be made before a ship was at last able to penetrate the ice that surrounded the island. When they were finally picked up, the men were weak and close to death after having spent 20 weeks on the barren island during yet another Antarctic winter. Quite miraculously they all eventually recovered their strength.

Although the Imperial Trans-Antarctic Expedition had been a failure, the courage and endurance displayed by its members were remarkable. As a heroic achievement, it ranks with Mawson's lonely sledge journey and Scott's fateful polar trek.

Ernest Shackleton was back again in the Antarctic in 1921, this time on an expedition that was to map the unknown Antarctic coast south of the Indian Ocean. Before the expedition actually got underway from South Georgia Island, Shackleton collapsed from a sharp pain in his chest. Within hours, the man who had defied the force of two Antarctic winters was dead of a heart attack. He was buried on South Georgia Island, just a few miles from the rocky shore where he had landed in the *James Caird*.

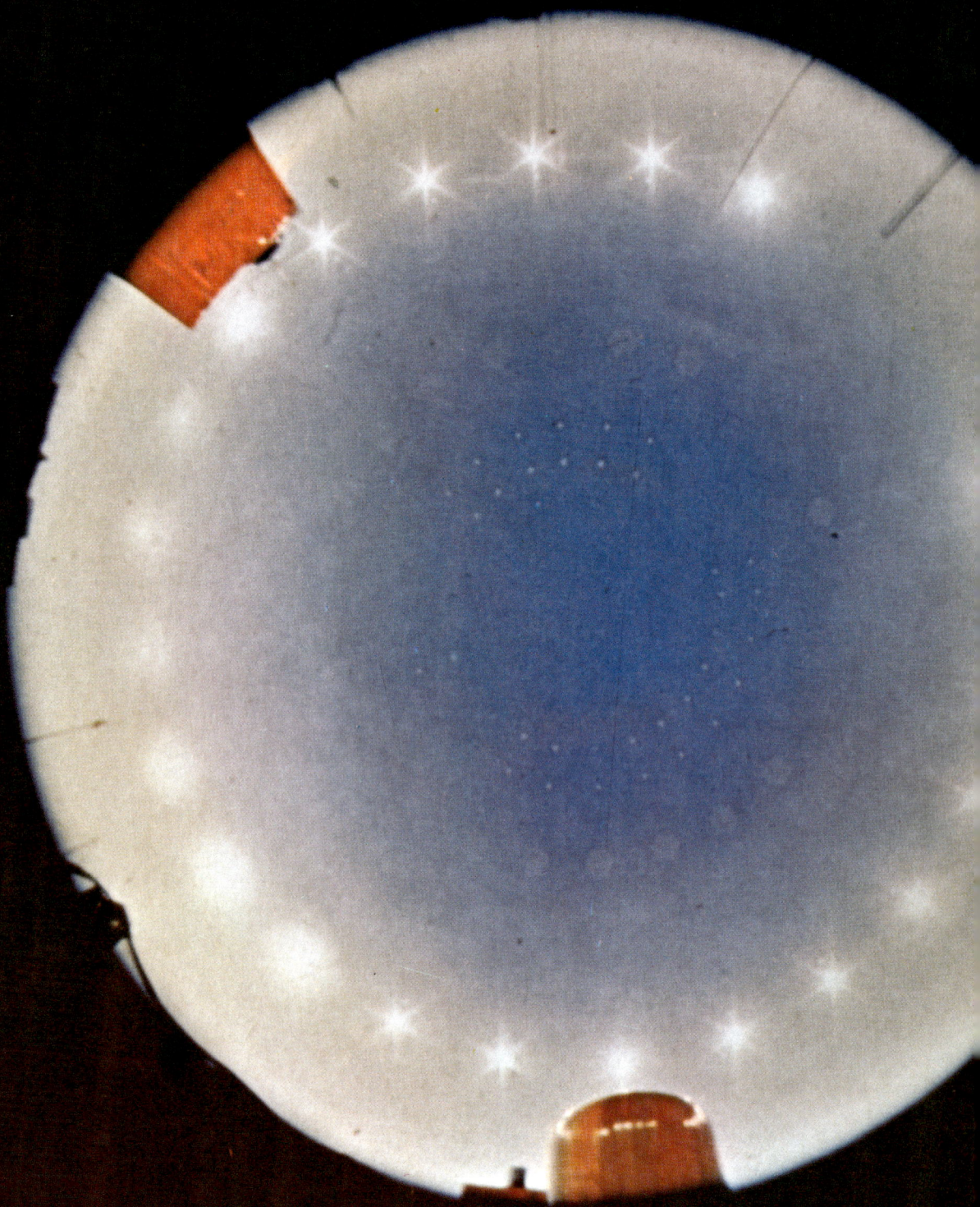

The Poles Today
11

Ernest Shackleton's death in January, 1922, marked the end of the heroic age of polar exploration. When this gay, adventurous, and supremely brave man succumbed to a heart attack the era of exploration with machines was about to begin. No longer would large expeditions make perilous journeys over the ice, carrying their equipment on sledges that they sometimes had to pull themselves.

Perhaps the most important new development in the machine-age conquest of the frozen worlds was the introduction of the airplane. In 1928, the Australian explorer and aviator Hubert Wilkins made the first flight over Antarctica. A year later, Commander Richard E. Byrd of the United States Navy became the first man to fly over the South Pole. Byrd was also the man responsible for the revival of American interest in Antarctic exploration. During the years between 1928–1930 he led an expedition that established an elaborate base of more than a dozen buildings at the Bay of Whales on the Ross Ice Shelf. This was in fact the first major American expedition to Antarctica since Charles Wilkes' voyage 80 years before. Byrd's equipment at Little America, as he called the base, included several airplanes, electricity, telephones, and three tall radio towers to keep in touch with the outside world. Four ships were needed to carry all the equipment and the 74 men to the "city" at Little America. During the first few years of their stay there the men were to carry out extensive geographical and geological work. Richard Byrd, meanwhile, prepared himself for the flight he and two other men were to make over the South Pole.

On November 29, 1929, they set out in their primitive plane to make polar history, thinking that they would follow the route Amundsen and his men had taken. But as the plane approached the icy mountains that separate the polar plateau from the Ross Ice Shelf, Byrd decided to follow the Liv Glacier. He knew that the highest point on the Heiberg Glacier that Amundsen had climbed was 10,500 feet. That would be too high for their overloaded plane to clear. The Liv, he hoped, would be lower.

Left: the sun in its clocklike "midsummer" orbit above the South Pole. An exposure was taken every hour for 22 hours by a camera with a fish-eye lens that had to be treated with special oils to protect it from icing up.

Above left: Richard E. Byrd, the first man to fly over the South Pole, taking a sighting. He, more than any other person, revived interest in the exploration of Antarctica.

Left: Byrd and Bennett returning from their flight over the North Pole in 1926. They had some trouble in navigating over the featureless white expanse of ice and snow, but the flight was otherwise not particularly eventful.

The plane was at full throttle as it climbed steadily and very slowly. Below them, the men could see the tumbled blocks of the glacier, and far ahead in the distance they could just make out the top of the pass. Suddenly the plane no longer responded to the controls. It climbed more and more slowly. Byrd shouted the order for 125 pounds of food (enough to last them for a week) to be pushed out of the plane. Now the aircraft began to climb again. The cliffs on each side of the pass were becoming so narrow that there was no hope of turning back. Another 125 pounds of food was jettisoned. If the plane crashed before their return to Little America, they would starve.

They were now approaching the top of the pass. After several agonizing moments of wondering whether they would actually clear it, the plane hummed over the icy peaks with a few hundred feet to spare. At last! Now they could relax and look down on the feature-less, snow-covered plain that leads to the pole.

Before returning to Little America they circled twice over the

Above: the Liv Glacier, photographed from an airplane that flew to the South Pole on the same route that Byrd followed on his way to the pole.

Above: Byrd cooking a meal on the stove that almost brought about his death during his lonely vigil in the weather station 123 miles from Little America. He was alone for more than four months in 1933 while the members of his second expedition continued their exploration of the unknown regions of Antarctica.

South Pole. Byrd dropped two flags out of the plane—the Stars and Stripes, and the Union Jack that he left in honor of Robert Scott and his men.

His next expedition to the Antarctic began in 1933, and wintered as before in the Bay of Whales at Little America. This expedition was primarily a scientific one and the men taking part in it studied meteors, cosmic rays, weather, geography, and the earth's magnetism. In order to take accurate and regular weather measurements, Byrd himself volunteered to man the isolated weather hut that was to be set up 123 miles from Little America. There was no room for three men in the lonely outpost and Byrd thought that two men would have difficulty getting along during the seven dark months of the Antarctic winter.

Sections of the prefabricated weather hut were damaged as they were dragged over the ice from Little America, and the door to the hut was so unevenly cut that it never closed completely. The hut itself was set into a pit with the door opening at the top, like a hatch. Some parts of Byrd's stove were missing. Although he tried to make do with repairing the stove himself, it was this essential item that nearly caused his death. Carbon monoxide leaked from the stove, and made him dizzy and sick. One day outside the hut he fell down and injured his arm. Yet throughout these trials he refused to ask the men at Little America for help. He felt that any rescue mission in mid-winter could involve the loss of lives.

As Byrd's radio transmissions became more incoherent, the men at Little America grew suspicious. Finally, against the orders he

Above: Mount Erebus, a live volcano, named for the ship of the Ross expedition, seen through the tail rotor of a helicopter. The photograph was taken on Operation Deep Freeze IV, the United States contribution to the International Geographical Year (1957–1958) in the Antarctic, of which Byrd was chief United States representative.

had given them, a small party set out for the weather hut. They used tractors to haul their supplies, but even so it took them a month to cover the 123 miles. Meanwhile the isolated man in the hut was spending many hours of each day only semi-conscious. The stove that was all that would keep him from freezing to death was also poisoning him.

At last, on August 11, after nearly five months of being alone in the Antarctic, Byrd saw the lights of the tractors approaching. He stood up but did not dare to walk forward. The men who had come to rescue him remember his greeting them and inviting them inside the hut for some hot soup. But Richard Byrd remembered nothing about this moment that was perhaps his narrowest escape from death. He was so weak that it was to be two months before he was

Above: Byrd Station, a United States base in Antarctica. Although it is only 5,000 feet above sea level, the ice has been measured at over 7,000 feet thick. Apparently the enormous weight of the icecap has pressed into the crust of the earth so that a large portion of the ice is below sea level.

well enough to be taken by plane back to the base at Little America.

Again in 1939, in 1946, and in 1957, Byrd was to return to the Antarctic. The 1946 expedition was the largest exploration of Antarctica ever attempted—Operation Highjump. Byrd had under his command 4,700 men and 13 ships. This great fleet was divided into three groups, which were assigned to various regions of the Antarctic. Fourteen hundred miles of unknown coastline were charted and photographed, new mountain ranges were discovered, and 26 new islands were found.

In 1955, Byrd was again in the Arctic, this time with Operation Deep Freeze, which was to be the basis for the United States participation in the International Geophysical Year. The IGY— involving 12 nations and 50 separate scientific bases on Antarctica—

Above: a Sno-cat tracked vehicle trapped in a crevasse during the 1957 British Commonwealth Trans-Antarctic Expedition. The photograph shows the light metal ramps that were placed under the vehicle. These, and the use of low gears, enabled the explorers to extricate the vehicle from a danger-ous situation.

began in July, 1957, and was the most productive scientific venture ever undertaken in the polar regions. The scientists who participated worked together to investigate things like the possible causes of earthquakes. Oceanography (oceans), meteorology (weather), the study of the sun's activity, and the earth's magnetism were some of the subjects they concentrated on. The most spectacular achievement of the IGY was the launching of artificial satellites and high-altitude rockets by Russia and the United States. These devices carried instruments to study cosmic

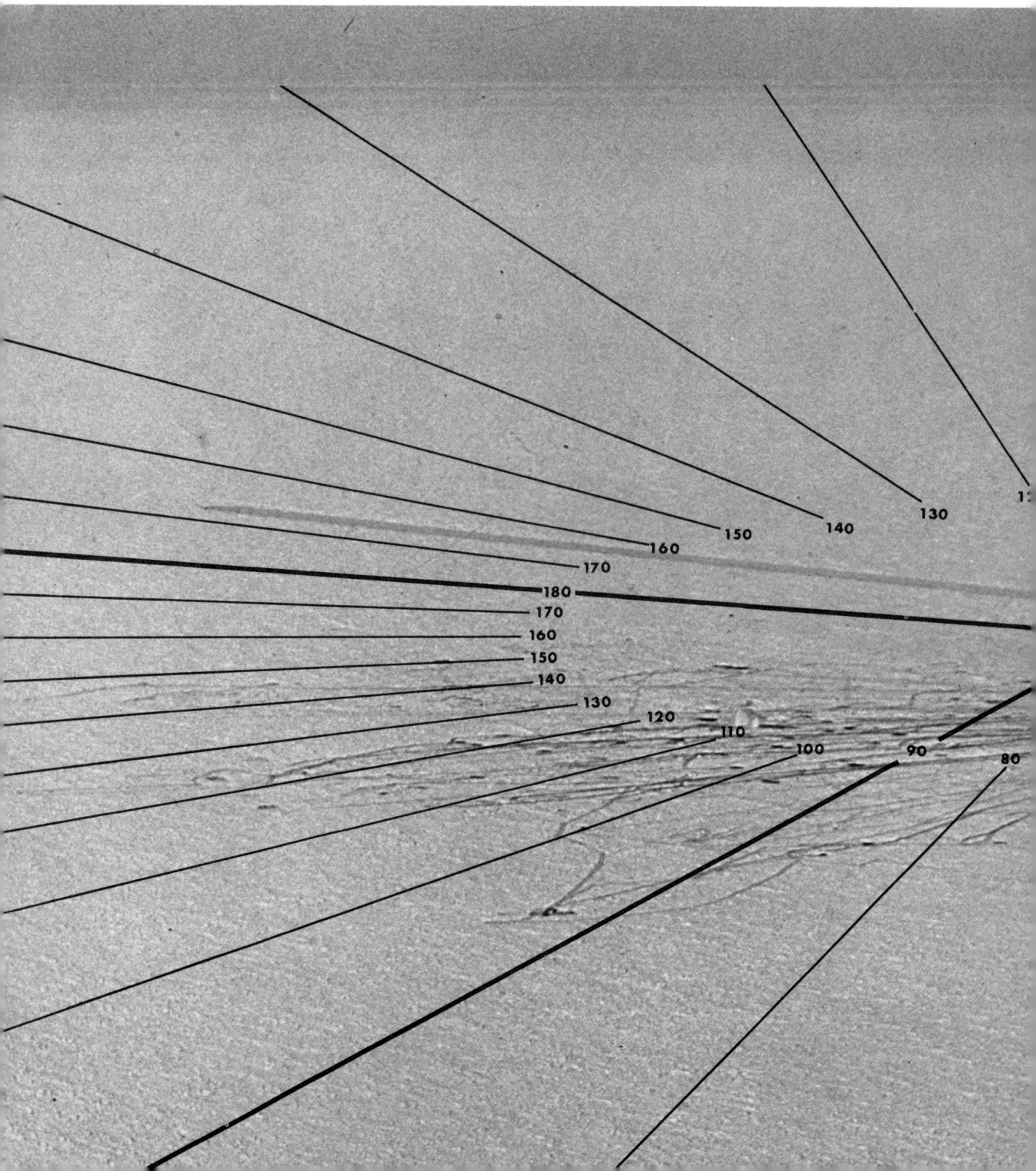

rays, magnetic fields, sunspots, eclipses, meteors, and sunlight.

The year of the IGY was also the time when Ernest Shackleton's dream was accomplished—the crossing of Antarctica from the Weddell Sea to the Ross Sea via the Pole. Early in October, 1957, a British explorer, Dr. Vivian Fuchs, who was the commander of the British Commonwealth Trans-Antarctic Expedition in 1957 and 1958, began breaking a trail toward the pole from his base camp on the Filchner Ice Shelf in the Weddell Sea. At the same time, the New Zealander Sir Edmund Hillary (who in 1953 had shared in the first

Below: the South Pole, photographed from an airplane by Emil Schulthess during the International Geophysical Year. Schulthess has superimposed a diagram that pinpoints the exact geographic pole (black dot at center) to within an area of about 30 feet in diameter. The lines drawn out from the pole are the meridians. The line at the right marked "0" is the Greenwich or Prime Meridian, which passes through Greenwich, England, and from which longitude is measured.

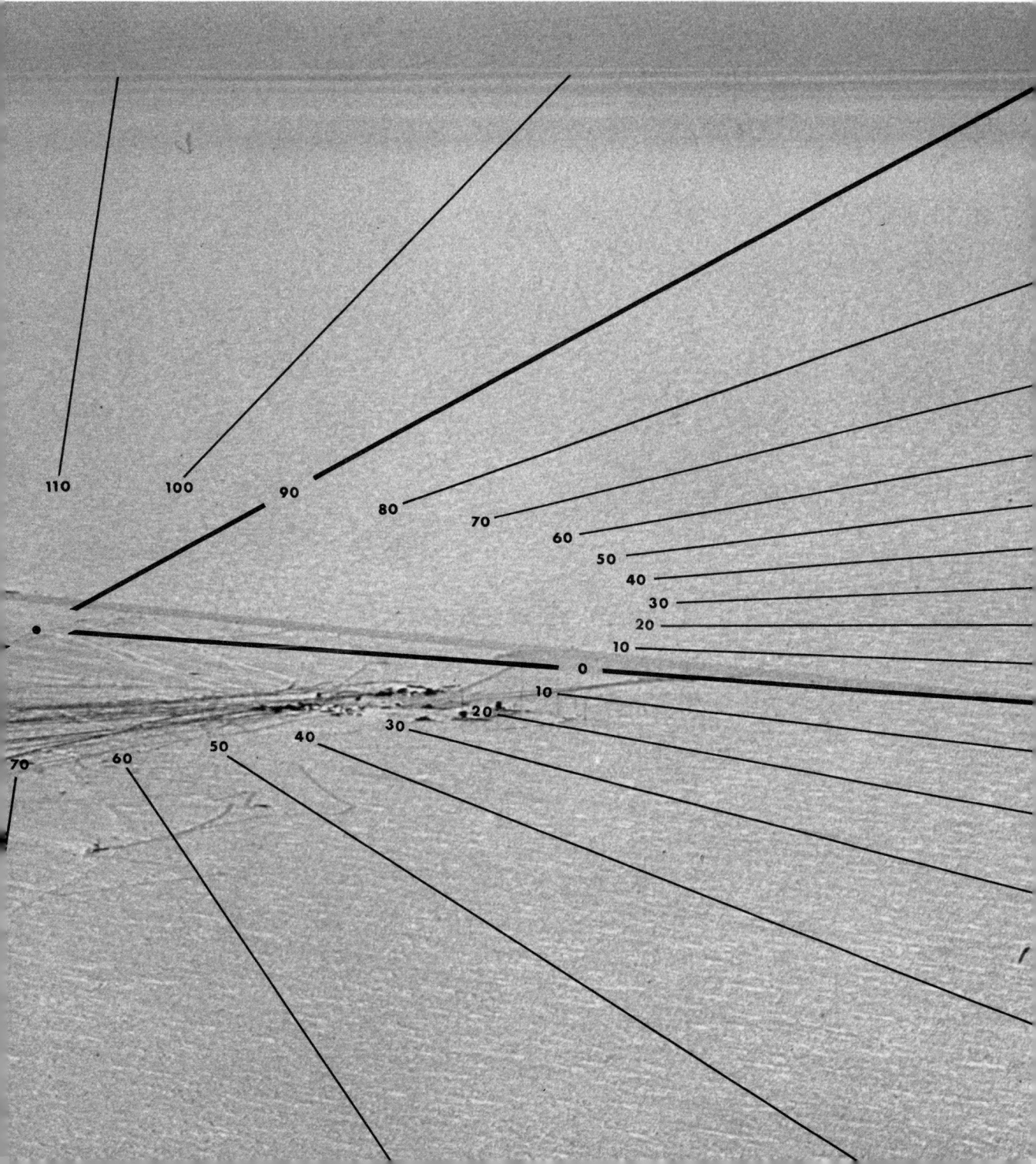

ascent of Mount Everest), and another group of men started pushing southward from their base on McMurdo Sound. Fuchs' plan was to trek across the entire continent via the South Pole and to get supplies from the depots that Hillary's party was to set up on the Ross Ice Shelf.

Even with large Sno-cats and Weasels, Fuchs and his men had a terrible struggle. The tractors were too cumbersome and were constantly getting stuck, as the snow bridges collapsed. Soon, they were behind schedule.

Below: Antarctica, showing the routes of explorers between 1928 and 1958. Also shown are the territories and bases of the numerous countries that have an interest in Antarctica today.

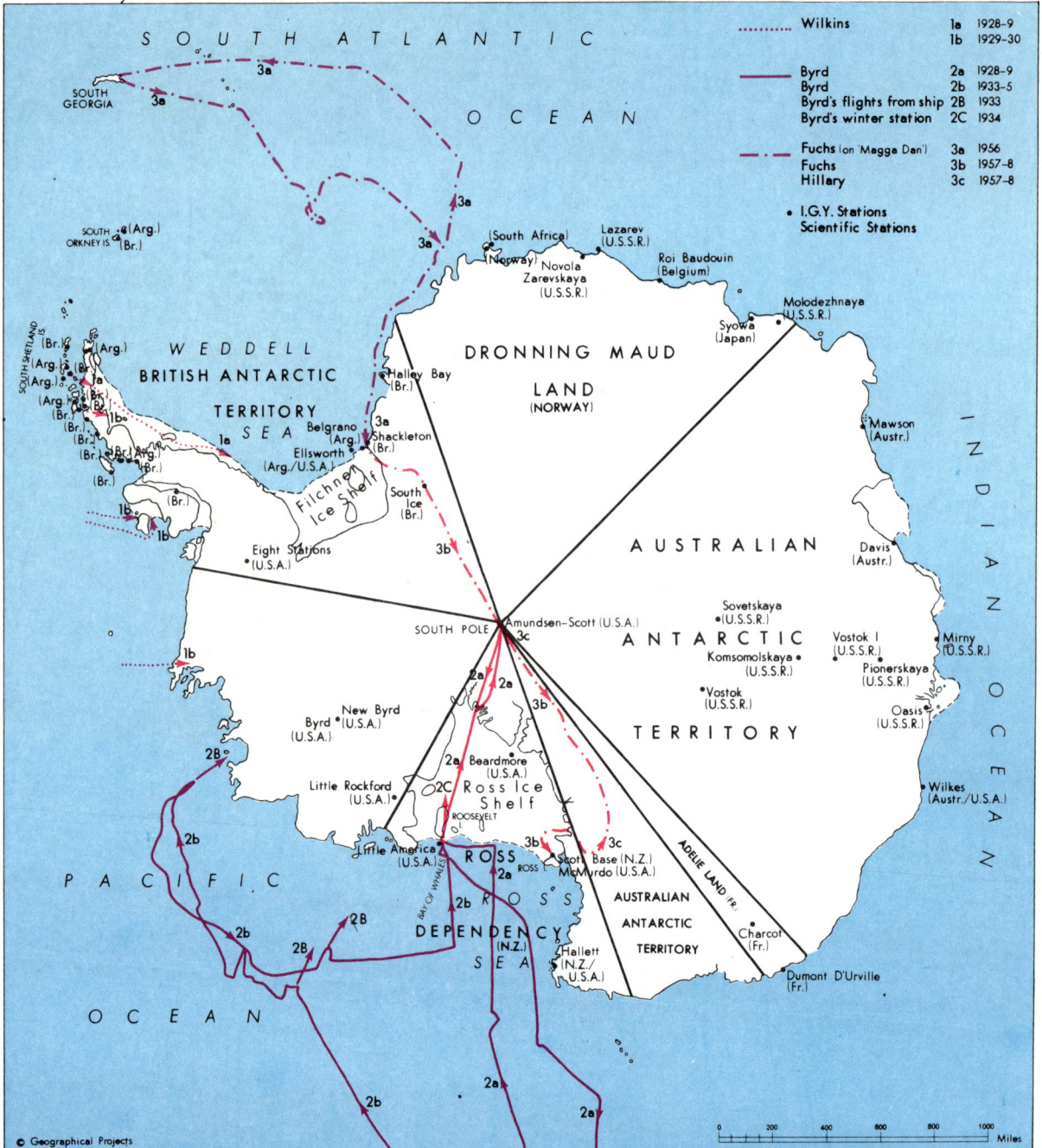

······ Wilkins	1a	1928-9
	1b	1929-30
—— Byrd	2a	1928-9
Byrd	2b	1933-5
Byrd's flights from ship	2B	1933
Byrd's winter station	2C	1934
—·—· Fuchs (on 'Magga Dan')	3a	1956
Fuchs	3b	1957-8
Hillary	3c	1957-8
• I.G.Y. Stations		
Scientific Stations		

SOUTH ATLANTIC OCEAN

SOUTH GEORGIA

SOUTH ORKNEY IS. (Arg.) (Br.)

SOUTH SHETLAND IS.

WEDDELL SEA

BRITISH ANTARCTIC TERRITORY

Halley Bay (Br.)

Belgrano (Arg.)
Ellsworth (Arg./U.S.A.)
Shackleton (Br.)
South Ice (Br.)

Filchner Ice Shelf

Eight Stations (U.S.A.)

(South Africa) (Norway)
Lazarev (U.S.S.R.)
Novola Zarevskaya (U.S.S.R.)
Roi Baudouin (Belgium)

Molodezhnaya (U.S.S.R.)
Syowa (Japan)

DRONNING MAUD LAND (NORWAY)

Mawson (Austr.)

AUSTRALIAN

Davis (Austr.)

SOUTH POLE
Amundsen-Scott (U.S.A.)

Sovetskaya (U.S.S.R.)
Komsomolskaya (U.S.S.R.)
Vostok (U.S.S.R.)

ANTARCTIC

Vostok I (U.S.S.R.)
Mirny (U.S.S.R.)
Pionerskaya (U.S.S.R.)
Oasis (U.S.S.R.)

New Byrd
Byrd (U.S.A.)

TERRITORY

Wilkes (Austr./U.S.A.)

Little Rockford (U.S.A.)

Beardmore (U.S.A.)
Ross Ice Shelf
ROOSEVELT

Little America (U.S.A.)

ROSS SEA
Scott Base (N.Z.)
McMurdo (U.S.A.)
ROSS

BAY OF WHALES

PACIFIC OCEAN

ROSS DEPENDENCY (N.Z.)

Hallett (N.Z./U.S.A.)

AUSTRALIAN ANTARCTIC TERRITORY

ADELIE LAND (Fr.)

Charcot (Fr.)

Dumont D'Urville (Fr.)

INDIAN OCEAN

© Geographical Projects

0 200 400 600 800 1000 Miles

Right: a Sno-cat carrying a crevasse detector: four wooden beams, fitted with large aluminum disks, pushed ahead of the vehicle. They are linked to detectors, which record hollows under the disks on a graph and also make a sound. As soon as a crevasse is discovered the Sno-cat must stop. Despite all precautions, the tractors still break through snow bridges. The surest way—although the slowest—is still a man probing with a metal rod.

Right: a Soviet tractor at Vostok Station in Antarctica. The southern continent is the most international of all, with the hostilities found in the rest of the world suspended for the sake of scientific research. Each year the Russian and American teams exchange a scientist, and many of the expeditions are organized jointly.

Hillary, meanwhile, was having much better luck. With his modified farm tractors, he pushed along at a good pace and was soon ahead of schedule. The original plan had been for Hillary to meet Fuchs at Depot 700, which was only 500 miles from the pole. But when Fuchs radioed that he was behind schedule, Hillary decided to push on to the south.

On January 3, 1958, he and his four companions reached the end of the earth, radioing, "Have hit the Pole bang on." This time a New Zealander had beaten an Englishman to the Pole. Then an argument ensued between the two expedition leaders that would never have occurred if the men had not had short-wave radios to communicate with each other. Because summer was almost over Hillary said to Fuchs and to the expedition authorities in London that Fuchs should abandon his transcontinental trip once he had reached the pole. From there his men and equipment could be flown out to McMurdo.

Fuchs was furious and radioed back that he had no intention of giving up on the last leg of the trip from the Pole to McMurdo Station. Dissention had reached Antarctica. Eventually, through the intervention of the London authorities, it was agreed that Fuchs should continue even though it meant danger. Hillary bowed to their decision and was there to shake Fuchs' hand when he arrived at the South Pole.

Despite the difficulties, Fuchs and his men completed their trek to McMurdo Sound on March 2, 1958—44 years after Shackleton had set out with the ill-fated Imperial Trans-Antarctic Expedition.

There are today more than 50 scientific stations scattered over Antarctica. Hundreds of men—and a few women—still explore there during the short summer from October to March. They keep in touch with one another and the outside world by radio and airplane. At several bases they can even see a movie during their leisure hours. A nuclear power generator operates from the huge American base at McMurdo Sound. Tourist ships now stop there. Today, rescue almost anywhere in Antarctica is only days away.

Thus the last great land mass to be discovered on earth has slowly been revealed and conquered. By the end of this century, geologists,

Above left: a painting of Amundsen's airship the *Norge* over Oslo on its way to the North Pole in April, 1926. Amundsen, and his Italian pilot Umberto Nobile, successfully crossed the pole in May 1926 a few days after Byrd flew over the South Pole.

Above and right: the airship *Italia*, in which Nobile (seen on left in group picture) set out to cross the North Pole two years later. For six weeks nothing was heard from the expedition, and Nobile and his crew were believed dead. Amundsen set out in an airplane with five others to search for him. A short time after they left, Nobile was found alive by another rescue expedition, having survived a crash. But Amundsen and his companions were never seen again.

meteorologists, geophysicists, and other scientists will have discovered more about how our weather is affected by the weather conditions in Antarctica. They will have mapped the land buried beneath its burden of ice, revealed its geological history, and systematically studied the oceans that surround the continent. Satellites in space will be monitoring Antarctic weather conditions and commercial airlines will be taking the southern circle route across its frozen wastes. Inevitably some kinds of industries will be set up in Antarctica.

Most important to the future of Antarctica is its unique status of being the only free continent on earth. A treaty ratified by 12 nations in 1959 guaranteed that no country would be able to exclude any other from performing peaceful or scientific experiments there.

In the Arctic during the 1900's the airplane also replaced the old methods of travel. Before his flight over the South Pole, Richard Byrd and Floyd Bennett became the first men to fly over the North Pole. In about 16 hours they made the round trip journey up and back again to Spitzbergen. Among those on hand to witness their return was Roald Amundsen who had hoped to make the first flight over the pole in the dirigible *Norge*. Three days after Bennett and Byrd had returned he took off in the *Norge* accompanied by an American, Lincoln Ellsworth, and Umberto Nobile of Italy. They completed a perilous flight from Spitzbergen over the pole and on to Alaska.

Another quite different attempt at a transpolar crossing occurred in 1931. This was the attempt by Sir Hubert Wilkins to cross the Arctic Ocean in his submarine the *Nautilus*. Although he failed to do this because of violent storms and damage to diving gear, Wilkins did much to promote the idea of under-ice navigation. However, nearly 30 years were to pass before the U.S. submarine *Nautilus* propelled by atomic power actually achieved the first under-ice crossing. Submerging under the ice off Point Barrow, the *Nautilus* traveled the 1,830 miles to a point near Spitzbergen in only 96 hours.

There nevertheless remains a certain attraction about polar expeditions that involve more than the use of machines to get men safely over the ice. On February 21, 1968, an Englishman, Wally Herbert, and three companions set out from Point Barrow, Alaska to cross the frozen Arctic Ocean on foot. Quite rightly they realized that this could be done only by the marriage of the oldest techniques of Arctic travel with modern air support,

Above: a member of Wally Herbert's Trans-Arctic Expedition with a dog sledge, traveling over good ice. The party left Point Barrow in February, 1968, and arrived north of Spitzbergen in May, 1969, having come over the pole.

Below: members of the Herbert team maneuvering their dogs over an ice ridge. The last part of the journey was a race against time, knowing that they had to reach Spitzbergen before the summer came and the ice began to melt.

radios, and satellite information on weather and ice concentration. They reached the North Pole on April 6, 1969, and from there proceeded in forced marches of 15 hours each in order to reach Spitzbergen before the summer melt of the ice. They had to make speed in order to save their lives, and on June 11, 1969, reached Spitzbergen—3,700 miles from their starting point and 476 days later.

Increasingly, however, emphasis has changed from exploration to economics in the Arctic. The rivalry between various nations to find a Northwest Passage or to be first at the pole has evolved into economic competition with Russia, the United States, and Canada being the principal competitors. The two superpowers, Russia and the United States, confront each other across the Bering Strait only minutes away from each other by rocket. The smaller nations of the Arctic region also claim their triangular wedges of territory extending northward to the Pole. The Soviet Union makes even more sweeping claims. In her sector—nearly half of all the Arctic region—the U.S.S.R. claims control of the sea with its floating ice islands and even the air routes above the ocean itself.

Below: the vast oil tanker, the S.S. *Manhattan,* plows stolidly through the ice during a double voyage through the Northwest Passage in 1969 to test the possibility of carrying oil from the Alaskan fields through this route.

Above: McMurdo Station, Ross Island.
It is the largest Antarctic station,
with a summer population of 1,000.
It has a nuclear reactor to provide
heat and electricity, such amenities
as a bowling alley and a newspaper
called the *McMurdo Sometimes*, and a
church named the Chapel of the Snows.

The discovery of huge new deposits of oil along the Arctic coast of Alaska has disturbed relations between Canada and the United States. An international oil company has successfully sent an ice-breaking tanker on a round-trip voyage through the Northwest Passage to test the possibility of transporting oil along this northern route. But the Passage cuts through the islands claimed by Canada, which regards this territory—land and sea—as her own. If one of the giant tankers planned for the Northwest Passage were to sink or be damaged by ice, the oil spewed over the icy water would completely destroy the animal and plant life in the Arctic. An oil pipeline that will run between Anchorage, Alaska, and the northern oilfields may seriously disrupt the delicate balance of life in the tundra. Already, parts of northern Canada and Alaska have been marred by the construction of drilling towers and the massive pieces of equipment used by the oil companies. An influx of people employed in the search for oil and other minerals has drastically changed the life of the Eskimo. They were quick to adapt themselves to a more mechanized way of life and are forgetting the hunting and fishing skills that enabled them to survive for so long in their hostile environment.

The future of the Arctic, like the Antarctic, remains very much an open question. With the successful construction of nuclear power plants man could live the year round in many parts of both polar regions. The possibility of establishing polar colonies where food could be grown and animals could be raised is still extremely remote. Seventy years ago man had not yet managed to get to the poles. Nor, certainly, had he any idea of the potential wealth of the natural resources surrounding them. The next stage in the evolution of the frozen world may be settlement.

Appendix

This appendix contains a necessarily small selection of quotations from the wealth of original firsthand material recording the exploits and impressions of the polar explorers. From the time of Pytheas in 330 B.C. almost all of the travelers to the frozen worlds left some written account of their journeys. For over 1,000 years they did not know the size of these regions or what was in them. Gradually, by the time of the merchant adventurers in the 1500's, explorers had learned more about the earth and the Arctic. Men such as Willem Barents set out in search of a route to the Orient only to find their ships frozen into impassable ice.

Attempts to find a Northeast or Northwest Passage to the Far East continued for nearly 500 years. By the early 1800's, there were large naval expeditions, which showed amazing fortitude and suffered from incredibly bad luck. After Sir John Franklin and his two ships disappeared during the years between 1845 and 1848, there followed nearly 20 years of exploration in the Arctic directed at finding the missing Franklin men.

Then in the 1900's, both the geographic poles were reached. Although disaster and drama were never far away, as witnessed by Robert F. Scott and Richard E. Byrd, this was the period when man learned how to survive in the polar regions.

Capsule biographies of the explorers are included in the second part of the appendix, arranged in alphabetical order for quick and easy reference. Maps in the same section show the routes followed by explorers not previously mapped in the book.

The glossary that follows the biographies gives a full explanation of terms used in the book and definitions of unusual words and phrases. Index and credit information complete the appendix.

Above: Fridtjof Nansen and his companion Hjalmar Johansen as they set off from the *Fram* with dogs, sledges, and kayaks to reach the North Pole.

Beware of CO

One of the problems faced by explorers who have camped in the polar regions has been the difficulty of keeping warm and at the same time avoiding carbon-monoxide poisoning. The first reported instance of this was in December, 1596. Willem Barents and his men were suffering from the cold. A freezing northeasterly wind blew over their camp on Novaya Zemlya, and by December 7, they could endure the cold no longer:

"The 7 of December it was still foule weather, and we had a great storme with a north-east wind, which brought an extreme cold with it; at which time we knew not what to do, and while we sate consulting together what were best for us to do, one of our companions gave us counsell to burne some of the sea-coles that we had brought out of the ship, which would cast a great heat and continue long; and so at evening we made a great fire thereof, which cast a great heat. At which time we were very careful to keepe it in, for that the heat being so great a comfort unto us, we tooke care how to make it continue long; whereupon we agreed to stop up all the doores and the chimney, thereby to keepe in the heate, and so went into our cabans to sleepe, well comforted with the heat, and so lay a great while talking together; but at last we were taken with a great swounding and daseling in our heads, yet some more then other some, which we first perceived by a sick man and therefore the lesse able to beare it, and found our selves to be very ill at ease, so that some of us that were strongest start out of their cabans, and first opened the chimney and then the doores, but he that opened the doore fell downe in a swound with much groaning uppon the snow; which I hearing, as lying in my caban next to the doore, start up and there saw him lying in a swoon, and casting vinegar in his face recovered him againe, and so he rose up. And when the doores were open, we all recovered our healthes againe by reason of the cold aire; and so the cold, which before had been so great enemy unto us, was then the onely reliefe that we had, otherwise without doubt we had all died in a sodaine swound. After that, the master . . . gave every one of us a little wine to comfort our hearts.

Gerrit de Veer's narrative in Three Voyages by the Northeast Vol. 13 *Hakluyt Society (London: 1853). Reprinted with the permission of Cambridge University Press.*

Above: a decorative pitcher, one of many articles found 274 years after Willem Barents and his men had spent the winter on Novaya Zemlya.

Above right: the polar bears were a constant menace to Barents and his men. Here one man is being devoured by a bear, while another Dutchman from the group tries to shoot it.

Right: the hut used by Barents and his men. It is easy to see from this engraving that proper ventilation of the hut must have been a great problem.

The Amazing Amateur

In May, 1860, an American with no experience as an explorer and no scientific knowledge set out to solve the mystery of the missing Franklin expedition. This was Charles Francis Hall, a poor but ambitious printer from Cincinnati, who believed that by going and living among the Eskimos he would discover the fate of the still missing men from the Franklin expedition. Although he found no relics of the Franklin mission during his first journey, Hall again set out for the Arctic in July 1864. This time he was to spend five years with the Eskimos in the region of the Melville Peninsula. In late spring 1869 he sledged across the Rae Isthmus to King William Island where he found many relics of the Franklin expedition. Here are excerpts from a letter he wrote to one of his backers.

"The result of my sledge journey to King William's Land may be summed up thus: None of Sir John Franklin's companions ever reached or died on Montreal Island. It was late in July 1848 that Crozier [who took command of the expedition after Sir John Franklin's death] and his party of about forty or forty-five passed down the west coast of King William's Land in the vicinity of Cape Herschel. The party was dragging two sledges on the sea-ice which was nearly in its last stage of dissolution. . . . Just before Crozier and party arrived at Cape Herschel they were met by four families of natives and both parties went into camp near each other. Two Eskimo men who were of the native party gave me much sad but deeply interesting information. Some of it stirred my heart with sadness intermingled with rage for it was a confession that they with their companions did secretly and hastily abandon Crozier and his party to suffer and die for need of fresh provisions.

"I tried hard to accomplish far more than I did but not one of the company would on any account whatever consent to remain with me in that country and make a summer search over that island. . . . Knowing as I now do the character of the Eskomos in that part of the country in which King William's Land is situated I cannot wonder at nor blame the Repulse Bay natives for their refusal to remain there as I desired. It is quite probable that had we remained there as I wished no one of us would ever have got out of the country alive. How could we expect if we got into straitened circumstances that we would receive better treatment from the

Above: a portrait of Charles Francis Hall. Like many explorers of the 1850's and 1860's, he was determined to solve the mystery of the missing Franklin.

Below: a portrait of Sir John Franklin painted shortly after the second expedition that he led to the Arctic.

Left: in the summer of 1871, Hall commanded another Arctic expedition, which sailed in a ship called *Polaris*. This sketch shows one of the crewmen trying to anchor the ship to an iceberg during a winter gale.

Below: Early in November, 1871, Hall became seriously ill from severe stomach pains and died aboard the *Polaris*. Almost 100 years later Hall's perfectly preserved body was dug up off the northwest coast of Greenland. An investigation proved conclusively that Hall's stomach pains had been brought on by poison. The mystery of why his crewmen should wish to kill him will never be solved.

Eskimos of that country than the 105 souls who were under the command of the heroic Crozier some time after landing on King William's Land? . . . the remains of nearly 100 of his [Franklin's] companions . . . lie about the places where the three boats have even been found and at the large camping-place at the head of Terror Bay and the three other places that I have already mentioned. . . . The native who conducted my native party in its search over King William's Land is the same individual who gave Dr. Rae the first information about white men having died to the westward of where he [Dr. Rae] then was [Pelly Bay] in the spring of 1854. . . . He is, in fact, a walking history of the fate of Sir John Franklin's Expedition . . . after stopping a few days among his people, he accompanied me to the places I visited on and about King William's Land.

"I could have readily gathered great quantities—a very great variety—of RELICS of Sir John Franklin's Expedition, for they are now possessed by natives all over the Arctic Regions that I visited or heard of—from Pond's Bay to Mackenzie River. As it was, I had to be satisfied with taking upon our sledges about 125 pounds total weight of relics from natives about King William's Land. . . ."

Narrative of the Second Arctic Expedition Made by C. F. Hall *ed. by J. E. Nourse (Trubner & Co: London, 1879) pp. 415–418.*

The Color of the North

Of all the polar explorers Fridtjof Nansen seems the most exceptional—a man whose achievements extended beyond those of exploration. He was a distinguished scientist whose organizing ability and willpower were demonstrated by the success of the Fram expedition (1893–1896). His humanitarian work with prisoners of war in World War I resulted in his receiving the Nobel Peace Prize in 1922. In his writings we glimpse other aspects of his personality—those of the artist and poet.

Above: Fridtjof Nansen, who conceived the idea of drifting over the polar icecap in a boat designed to withstand great pressure from the ice.

"I wandered about over the floe towards evening. Nothing more wonderfully beautiful can exist than the Arctic night. It is dreamland, painted in the imagination's most delicate tints; it is colour etherealised. One shade melts into the other, so that you cannot tell where one ends and the other begins, and yet they are all there. No forms—it is all faint, dreamy colour music, a far-away, long-drawnout melody on muted strings. Is not all life's beauty high, and delicate, and pure like this night? Give it bright colours, and it is no longer so beautiful. The sky is like an enormous cupola, blue at the zenith, shading down into green, and then into lilac and violet at the edges. Over the ice-fields there are cold violet-blue shadows, with

Above: a cartoon from the newspaper *Framsjaa* produced on board the *Fram*. This one concerns a joke about some boots designed by the ship's captain.

lighter pink tints where a ridge here and there catches the last reflection of the vanished day. Up in the blue of the cupola shine the stars, speaking peace, as they always do, those unchanging friends. In the south stands a large red-yellow moon, encircled by a yellow ring and light golden clouds floating on the blue background. Presently the aurora borealis shakes over the vault of heaven its veil of glittering silver—changing now to yellow, now to green, now to red. It spreads, it contracts again, in restless change, next it breaks into waving, many-folded bands of shining silver, over which shoot billows of glittering rays; and then the glory vanishes. Presently it shimmers in tongues of flame over the very zenith; and then again it shoots a bright ray right up from the horizon, until the whole melts away in the moonlight, and it is as though one heard the sigh of a departing spirit. Here and there are left a few waving streamers of light, vague as a foreboding—they are the dust from the aurora's glittering cloak. But now it is growing again; new lightnings shoot up; and the endless game begins afresh. And all the time this utter stillness, impressive as the symphony of infinitude."

Farthest North Vol. 1 *F. Nansen (Archibald Constable and Company: London, 1955) pp. 220–221.*

Left: Nansen and his sledge. Because of the strong wind, he and Johansen rigged sails over their sledges. Then they stood on their skis in front, holding on to a projecting pole.

Right: a drawing that shows the difficulties of handling sledge dogs. In October, 1893, Nansen tried his hand at dog driving and quickly realized that he had not yet mastered the technique.

The Cook-Peary Controversy

Left: Dr. Frederick A. Cook became known both as a mountaineer and as an explorer. During the years 1903–1906 he led expeditions to ascend Mount McKinley in Alaska. His claim to have been to the top was doubted because of the testimony of the men who had taken part in earlier attempts on the summit.

Right: Peary's American flag at the pole. After this photograph was taken the flag was cut so that a diagonal strip could be left at the North Pole. Today Peary's patched flag is in the Explorers' Hall of the National Geographical Society in Washington.

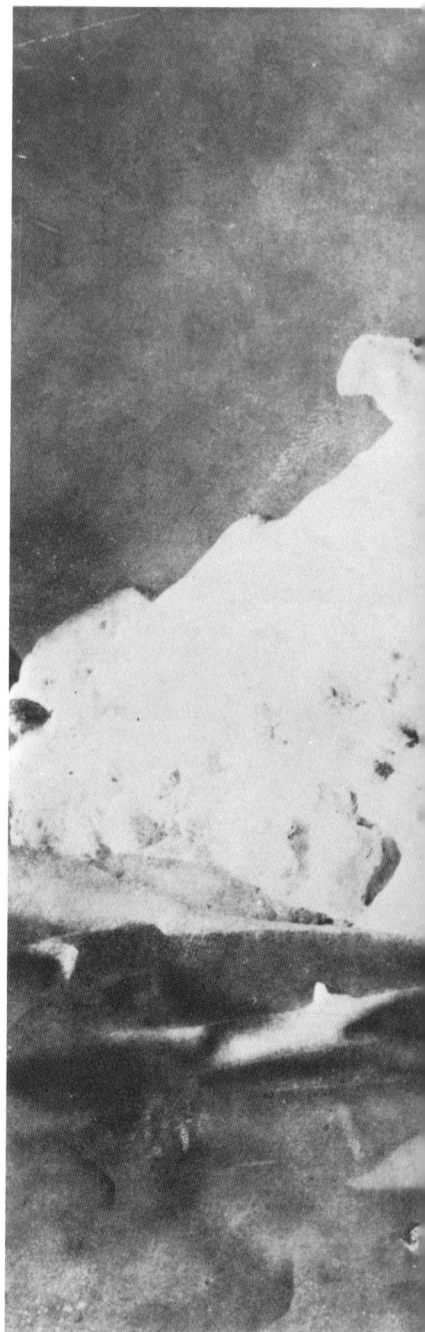

On September 7, 1909, Robert Peary announced to the world his achievement of having conquered the Geographical North Pole. Five days earlier another American, Dr. Frederick Cook, had announced that he had got there with two Eskimo companions in April 1908. Cook had experience as an explorer and a mountaineer and in 1892 he had accompanied Peary to Greenland. His claim of having been first at the pole was challenged by Peary and cross-questioned by the geographical societies in the United States and Britain. In November, 1909, a panel of experts for the National Geographic Society reported its opinion that Peary had reached the pole first. Nevertheless, the mystery remained open for the next 20 years with supporters of both Peary and Cook accusing each of the explorers of having made false claims. Peary remained the declared conquerer of the North Pole while Frederick Cook became known as the man who made up a story about his conquest.

"APPENDIX III
REPORT OF THE SUB-COMMITTEE OF THE NATIONAL GEOGRAPHIC SOCIETY ON PEARY'S RECORDS AND SOME OF THE HONOURS AWARDED FOR THE ATTAINMENT OF THE POLE.

"The Board of Managers of the National Geographic Society at a meeting held at Hubbard Memorial Hall, November 4, 1909, received the following report:

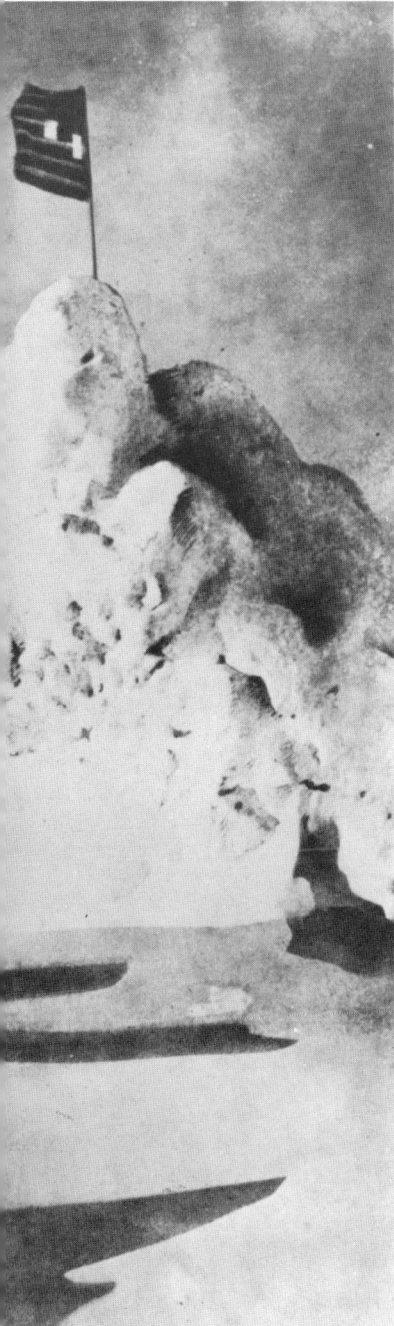

"The sub-committee to which was referred the task of examining the records of Commander Peary in evidence of his having reached the North Pole, beg to report that they have completed their task.

"Commander Peary has submitted to his sub-committee his original journal and records of observations, together with all his instruments and apparatus, and certain of the most important of the scientific results of his expedition. These have been carefully examined by your sub-committee, and they are unanimously of the opinion that Commander Peary reached the North Pole on April 6, 1909.

"They also feel warranted in stating that the organization, planning, and management of the expedition, its complete success, and its scientific results, reflect the greatest credit on the ability of Commander Robert E. Peary, and render him worthy of the highest honours that the National Geographic Society can bestow upon him. HENRY GANNETT, C. M. CHESTER, O. H. TITTMAN.

"Among the honours awarded for the attainment of the Pole are the following:

The Special Great Gold Medal of the National Geographic Society of Washington.

The Special Great Gold Medal of the Royal Geographical Society of London.

The Nachtigall Gold Medal of the Imperial German Geographical Society.

The Hauer Medal of the Imperial Austrian Geographical Society.

The Cook-Peary Controversy

Left: Robert Peary on board the *Roosevelt* after his successful conquest of the North Pole.

The King Humbert Gold Medal of the Royal Italian Geographical Society.

The Gold Medal of the Hungarian Geographical Society.

The Gold Medal of the Royal Belgian Geographical Society.

The Gold Medal of the Royal Geographical Society of Antwerp.

A Special Trophy from the Royal Scottish Geographical Society—a replica in silver of the ships used by Hudson Baffin and Davis.

The Helen Culver Medal of the Chicago Geographical Society.

The Special Gold Medal of the Philadelphia Geographical Society.

The Honorary Degree of Doctor of Laws from the Edinburgh University.

The Honorary Degree of Doctor of Laws from Bowdoin College.

Honorary Membership in the Manchester Geographical Society.

Honorary Membership in the Royal Netherlands Geographical Society of Amsterdam.

The North Pole Appendix III *Robert E. Peary (Hodder & Stoughton: London, 1910) pp. 313–315.*

Finding the North Pole

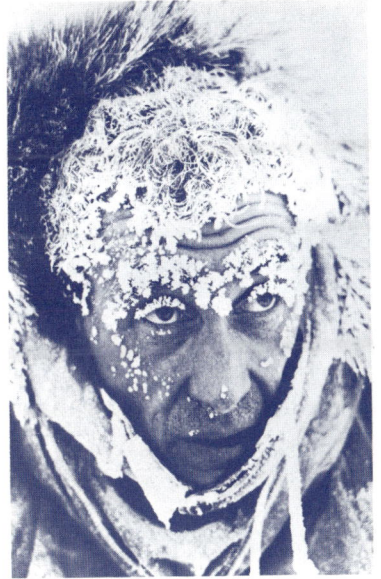

At 7 A.M. on April 5, 1969, Wally Herbert, leader of the four-man British Trans-Arctic Expedition sent a radio message to Queen Elizabeth announcing that he and his three companions had reached the North Pole. A few moments later he was shocked to find that they were in fact seven miles short of the pole instead of about a mile and a half. The difficulty of actually locating the top of the world is best explained in Wally Herbert's own words.

Above: Allan Gill one of the four men of the British Trans-Arctic Expedition.

"Navigation in the vicinity of the Pole is a problem. If your calculation of the longitude is slightly out, then the time at which the sun crosses your meridian—in other words that time at which the sun is due north—is wrong, and so you head in the wrong direction. And of course, if you head in the wrong direction, you increase your errors in your dead reckoning longitude. Your azimuth then is thrown even further into error and you increase your errors progressively until you spiral into almost a complete circle. This is what happened to us on this particular day.

"We set off and travelled for what we estimated was seven miles and stopped. We set up the theodolite, did a rough calculation, and

Below: an aerial photograph of the expedition making its way over tough ice in the Arctic.

Finding the North Pole

found that we were still seven miles from the Pole. It was unbelievable. We had used up a lot of our time in getting there—the G.M.T. date was going to change within the next seven hours and we were still seven miles short of our goal. We couldn't understand where we had gone wrong. How could one travel seven miles in the direction of the North Pole and still be seven miles from it? The only possible answer was that we must have been travelling parallel to the dateline and were thus passing the Pole. We concluded there must have been something very wrong with our azimuth taken from the position we had computed that morning; so we went into the computations again, and found an error in the longitude. We did another series of observations, all of which took time, and set off again. We travelled hard for three hours, set up a theodolite yet again, and found that we were three miles south of the Pole and on longitude zero. With Spitzbergen as our goal and being still three weeks behind schedule, we should really have carried straight on and not gone back.

"But one cannot with a clear conscience say one is at the Pole when one is three miles short of it – more especially since we had told Her Majesty that by dead reckoning we had reached it. So we set off yet again, travelling on a very precise azimuth. We chopped through every single pressure ridge that came our way, cutting ourselves a dead straight line due north. But it was slow progress and the drift was going against us. We were . . . hardly making any progress at all. After about four hours we'd come less than a mile.

"In desperation, we off-loaded the sledges, laid a depot and took on with us only the barest essentials, just enough for one night's camp. It was a risk, the only time during the whole journey that we took such a risk. But it paid off. With the lighter sledges we made faster progress, and after about three hours estimated that we must surely be at the Pole, possibly even beyond it. So we stopped, set up our tents, and did a final fix which put us at 89° 59′ N, one mile south of the North Pole on longitude 180. In other words, we'd crossed the Pole about a mile back along our tracks. But the drift was now with us, so we must surely cross the Pole a second time as we drifted overnight. We got into our sleeping-bags. . . .

"The pad marks of thirty-five Eskimo huskies, the broad tracks of four heavy Eskimo-type sledges, and the four sets of human footprints which had approached the North Pole and halted one mile

Right: killing a polar bear. Wally Herbert explained in his book that "this wasn't sport, this was the real thing. We were killing to protect ourselves and the dogs. . . ."

Above: the four members of the expedition after they had finally managed to get to the North Pole.

Left: Wally Herbert, who wanted to accomplish the only remaining pioneer journey on the earth—the trek across the top of the world.

beyond it on the morning of Easter Sunday, 1969, no longer mark the spot where we took our final sun shots and snatched a few hours' rest. For even while we were sleeping, our camp was slowly drifting; and the Pole, by the time we had reloaded our sledges a few hours later and set course of the island of Spitzbergen, lay north in a different direction.

"It had been an elusive spot to find and fix. At the North Pole, two separate sets of meridians meet and all directions are south. The temperature was minus 35° Fahrenheit. The wind was from the south-west, or was it from the north-east? It was Sunday, or was it Saturday? Maybe it was Monday. It was a confusing place to be—a place which lay on our course from Barrow to Spitzbergen and which had taken us 408 days to reach."

Trying to set foot upon it had been like trying to step on the shadow of a bird that was circling overhead. The surface across which we were moving was itself a moving surface on a planet that was spinning about an axis. We were standing approximately on that axis, asleep on our feet, dog tired and hungry. Too tired to celebrate our arrival on the summit of this super-mountain around which the sun circles almost as though stuck in a groove.

We set up our camera and posed for some pictures – thirty-six shots at different exposures. We tried not to look weary, tried not to look cold. We tried only to huddle, four fur-clad figures, in a pose that was vaguely familiar – for what other proof of the attainment could we bring back than a picture posed in this way?"

Across the Top of the World *W. Herbert (Longmans: London, 1969) pp. 172–174.*

Seal Hunting

In his numerous trips to the Arctic, Vilhjalmur Stefansson was continually impressed by the Eskimo methods of survival. To keep from starving the Eskimos had at all seasons of the year to exert their wits in hunting and fishing for food.

When he lived with the MacKenzie River people Stefansson had observed their very cunning way of hunting seal, based on their knowledge of the animals' psychology and habits. During the late spring and summer, seals emerge entirely from their holes and lie beside them to enjoy the warm sun. During these "sun-baths" the seals take short naps of a minute or two. Between these naps they raise their heads and take a survey of the horizon to see whether anyone is approaching.

"The whole principle of successfully stalking a seal is just in realizing from the first that he is bound to see you and that your only way is in pretending that you also are a seal. If you act and look so as to convince him from the first that you are a brother seal, he will regard you with unconcern. To simulate a seal well enough to fool a seal is not difficult, for, to begin with, we know from experience that his eye-sight is poor. You can walk up without taking any special precautions until, under ordinary conditions of light, you are within two hundred and fifty or three hundred yards. Then you have to begin to be more careful. You move ahead while he is sleeping and when he wakes up you stop, motionless. You can safely proceed on all fours until within something less than two hundred yards. . . . Your method of locomotion will then have to be that of the seal, which does not differ very materially from that of a snake, and which therefore has its disadvantages at a season of the year when the surface of the ice is covered with puddles of water anywhere from an inch to twenty inches in depth, as it is in spring and early summer. You must not only crawl ahead, seal-fashion, but you must be careful to always present a side view of your body to the seal. . . .

"Until you are within a hundred yards or so the seal is not likely to notice you, but somewhere between the hundred yard and the seventy-five yard mark his attention will suddenly be attracted to you, and instead of going to sleep, at the end of his ordinary short period of wakefulness, he will remain awake and stare at you steadily. The seal knows, exactly as well as the seal hunter knows, that no seal in this world will sleep continuously for as much as four minutes at a

Above: Vilhjalmur Stefansson who traveled to the Arctic with the simplest kind of equipment. In August 1906 he arrived at Herschel Island, about 200 miles north of the Arctic Circle, dressed in a summer weight suit. Stefansson wanted to learn from the Eskimos how to live in the Arctic.

Right: a photograph taken by Stefansson of a Mackenzie River Eskimo. During the winter of 1906–1907 the Mackenzie River people took Stefansson into their houses and treated him as an Eskimo.

time. If you lie still that long, he will know you are no seal, and up will go his tail and down he will slide into the water in the twnkling of an eye. When the seal, therefore, has been watching you carefully for twenty or thirty seconds, you must raise your head twelve or fifteen inches above the ice, look around seal-fashion so that your eyes will sweep the whole circle of the horizon, and drop your head again upon the ice. By the time he has seen you repeat this process two or three times in the space of five or six minutes he will be convinced that you are a seal, and all his worries will be gone. From then

Below: an engraving that shows an Eskimo hunter crawling up to a seal.

on you can proceed more rapidly, crawling ahead while he sleeps and stopping while he remains awake. . . . I have known of expert seal hunters who under emergencies would go after a seal without any ordinary weapon and crawl so near him that they could seize him by a flipper, pull him away from his hole, and club or stab him. My Eskimo companions generally used to crawl within about fifteen or twenty yards; but I have found under ordinary circumstances that fifty yards is close enough for a man with a rifle. The animal lies on a slippery incline beside his hole, so that the shot that kills him must kill him instantly. It must shatter the brain or break the spinal cord of the neck; the slightest quiver of a muscle will send him sliding into the water and all your work will have been to no purpose."

My Life with the Eskimo *V. Stefansson (Macmillan: London, 1913) pp. 109–110.*

175

Ponies in the Antarctic

During his South Pole attempt Robert F. Scott relied on Siberian ponies for hauling stores to the foot of the glacier leading to the polar plateau. There were motor sledges and Siberian huskies to haul the sledges as well, but Scott seems always to have had more faith in the ponies. In the following quotations we can see how much time and care was devoted to them. Perhaps Scott and his four companions would have survived their polar journey if they had relied more on the dogs and less on the ponies and their own strength to pull the sledges.

"*Friday, July 14.*—We have had a horrible fright and are not even yet out of the wood.

"At noon yesterday one of the best ponies, 'Bones,' suddenly went

Above: One of the motor sledges being landed from the *Terra Nova*. Soon after this picture was taken, the ice beneath the sledge gave way, and it disappeared.

Below: Scott (right) disembarking the ponies after the long sea voyage. They had suffered from skin irritations at sea and were eager to roll about on the ice and scratch themselves.

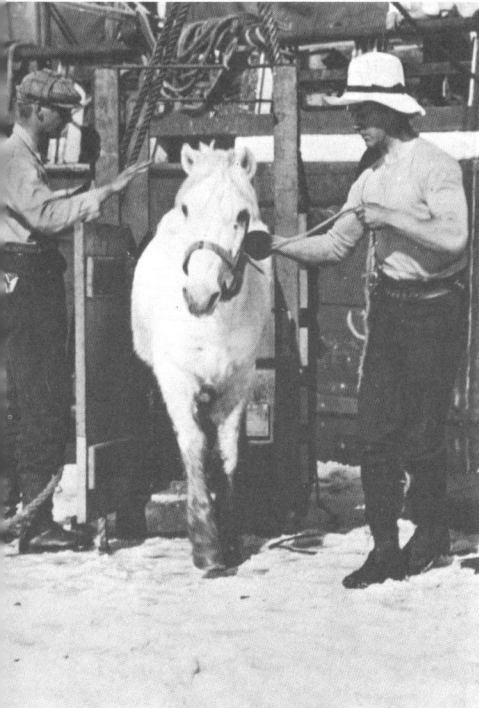

off his feed. . . . Every few minutes the poor beast had been seized with a spasm of pain, had first dashed forward as though to escape it and then endeavoured to lie down. Crean had had much difficulty in keeping him in, and on his legs, for he is a powerful beast. . . . Every now and again he attempted to lie down, and Oates eventually thought it was wiser to let him do so. Once down, his head gradually drooped until he lay at length, every now and again twitching very horribly with the pain and from time to time raising his head and even scrambling to his legs when it grew intense. I don't think I ever realised before how pathetic a horse could be under such conditions; no sound escapes him, his misery can only be indicated by those distressing spasms and by dumb movements of the head turned with a patient expression always suggestive of appeal. . . . Oates administered an opium pill and later on a second, sacks were heated in the oven and placed on the poor beast; beyond this nothing could be done except to watch. . . .

"It was shortly after midnight when I was told that the animal seemed a little easier. At 2.30 I was again in the stable and found the improvement had been maintained. . . . As I stood looking it suddenly raised its head and rose without effort to its legs; then in a moment, as though some bad dream had passed, it began to nose at some hay and at its neighbour. Within three minutes it had drunk a bucket of water and had started to feed.

"*Saturday, July 15.*—Oates thinks a good few of the ponies have got worms and we are considering means of ridding them. 'Bones' seems to be getting on well, though not yet quite so buckish as he was before his trouble. . . .

"*Wednesday, November 22.*—Camp 18. Everything much the same. The ponies thinner but not much weaker. The crocks still going along. Jehu [one of the ponies] is now called 'The Barrier Wonder' and Chinaman 'The Thunderboldt.' . . . Nobby keeps his pre-eminence of condition and has now the heaviest load by some 50 lbs.; most of the others are under 500 lbs. load, and I hope will be eased further yet. The dogs are in good form still, and came up well with their loads this morning (night temp. −1.4°). It looks as though we ought to get through to the Glacier without great difficulty. The weather is glorious and the ponies can make the most of their rest during the warmest hours, but they certainly lose in one way by marching at night. . . . We are quite steady on the march now, and though not fast yet get through with few stops. . . . There is rather an increased condition of false crust—that is, a crust which appears firm till the whole weight of the animal is put upon it, when it suddenly gives some three or four inches. This is very trying for the poor beasts.

"*Thursday, November 23.*—Camp 19. Getting along. I think the ponies will get through: we are now 150 geographical miles from the Glacier. But it is still rather touch and go. If one or more ponies were to go rapidly down hill we might be in queer street.

"*Tuesday, November 28.*—Camp 24. Chinaman, 'The Thunderboldt,'

Below: Captain Oates who was in charge of the ponies on the *Terra Nova*. Besides the four shown here, fifteen others were kept in the forecastle.

Ponies in the Antarctic

Above: giving whiskey to a pony that swam ashore from the *Terra Nova*.

Below: On the march to the South Pole. Already the ponies had begun to show signs of weakening.

has been shot to-night. Plucky little chap, he has stuck it out well and leaves the stage but a few days before his fellows. We have only four bags of forage (each one 30 lbs.) left, but these should give seven marches with all the remaining animals, and we are less than 90 miles from the Glacier. . . .

"Nobby was tried in snow-shoes this morning (Thursday, November 30) and came along splendidly on them for about four miles, then the wretched affairs racked and had to be taken off. There is no doubt that these snow-shoes are *the* thing for ponies, and had ours been able to use them from the beginning they would have been very different in appearance at this moment.

"*Tuesday, December 5.*—Camp 30. Noon. We awoke this morning to a raging, howling blizzard. The blows we have had hitherto have lacked the very fine powdery snow—that especial feature of the blizzard. To-day we have it fully developed. After a minute or two in the open one is covered from head to foot. . . . The ponies—head, tails, legs, and all parts not protected by their rugs—are covered with ice; the animals are standing deep in snow, the sledges are almost covered, and huge drifts above the tents.

"At 8 P.M. (Saturday, December 9) the ponies were quite done, one and all. They came on painfully slowly a few hundred yards at a time. By this time I was hauling ahead, a ridiculously light load, and yet finding the pulling heavy enough. We camped, and the ponies have been shot. Poor beasts! they have done wonderfully well considering the terrible circumstances under which they worked, but yet it is hard to have to kill them so early."

Scott's Last Expedition Vol. 1 *R. F. Scott et al. (Smith, Elder & Co: London, 1913) pp. 351–493.*

80° 08′ South

From noontime on March 28, until after midnight on August 11, 1934, Richard E. Byrd lived alone in an underground hut in the Antarctic at latitude 80° 08′ South. Quite suddenly, during the last days of May, he was struck down by symptoms he knew meant that he was being poisoned by carbon monoxide gas. At first he thought it was the gasoline engine that was leaking fumes, but the more Byrd thought about the leaky joints in the stove, the more he blamed it. He had to light the stove to keep himself warm—but this was his enemy. These are some of his recollections of the days he managed to live through during mid-July. By this time a rescue team had left Little America, hoping they would somehow manage to reach him despite the terrible winter weather conditions.

"On Saturday morning, after a dreadful night, I seemed again to be suspended in that queer, truncated borderland between sensibility and unconsciousness. It was all I could do to get up. When I threw the light on the thermograph, I saw that the red trace had twitched past 80° below zero at 3 o'clock in the morning, and had not risen. The boric acid which I used for washing out my eyes had burst its bottle. Even the milk in the thermos jar was frozen, and that part of the wall behind the stove which until then had resisted the rise of the ice was now covered with the white film. The skin came off my fingers as I fussed over the stove. I was too weak to stay on my feet; so I slumped into the sleeping bag. When I aroused, the time was nearly noon; I had missed the first radio schedule.

"At noon, and again on the 2 o'clock emergency schedule, I tried to regain touch with Little America. All I heard was the scraping of static. The thermograph trace held at 80° below zero, as if rigid in its track. I was beside myself with anxiety. At 4 o'clock, when nothing came out of my third attempt to raise the main base, I broadcast blind: 'Poulter, if still on the trail return to Little America. Await warmer weather.' Dyer did not hear it, but I had no way of knowing.

"My stomach would hold down nothing but hot milk. Most of the time I was screwed up in the sleeping bag, in a kind of daze. There was a fire in the stove all day; yet, the shack was almost unbearably cold. In the evening my senses revived; my eyes were smarting and running water; my head ached, and so did my back;

Above: Richard E. Byrd, the most important American polar explorer of the 1900's.

80° 08′ South

Right: view from the plane that Byrd and two other men flew to the South Pole on November 29, 1929.

and I realized that the room must be filling with fumes. So I forced myself out of the bunk to do whatever could be done. . . . The stovepipe, when I put my hand on it near the top, was cold; so it was clogged as well. And, realizing that I must somehow insulate it, I poked around in the veranda until I found a strip of asbestos. With this in my hand, and a piece of string, I climbed topside. The inside thermograph tracing showed 82° below zero—so cold that, when I opened the hatch, I couldn't breathe on account of the constriction of the breathing passages. The layer of air next to the surface must have been at least 84° below. Anyhow, I had to duck into the shack to catch my breath. Armed this time with the mask and holding my breath until I was out of the hatch, I started again for the stove-pipe. . . .

"A queer thing happened. I was on my knees, crawling. In one hand I had the flashlight, and on my back the asbestos. Half-way to the stovepipe, everything was blotted out. I thought at first the flashlight had gone out from the cold. But, when I looked up, I could not see the aurora. I was blind all right; the first thought was that my eyeballs were frozen. I groped back in the direction of the

Below: a ticker-tape welcome from New York City for Byrd after his first trip to Antarctica. This sort of parade is reserved for the nation's heroes—men such as General Eisenhower and Colonel John Glenn.

hatch, and presently my head collided with one of the steel guys anchoring the anemometer pole. I crouched there to think. I felt no pain. I took off my gloves and massaged the eye sockets gently. Little globules of ice clung to the lashes, freezing them together; when these came off, I could see again. But meanwhile the fingers of my right hand were frozen . . . and I had to slip the hand down into the crotch to warm them.

"I was a longish time wrapping the asbestos around the pipe. My mittened hands were clumsy and unsure. The pipe, I noticed, was choked with ice. The only opening was a little hole not much bigger than my thumb. Before I was done, my eyelashes froze again; this time I nipped two fingers of the left hand. In my hurry to get out of the cold I slid, rather than climbed, down the ladder. When I removed the mask, the skin came off my cheeks, just below the eyes. I was half an hour bringing life back into my fingers. . . .

"Weary as I was, I did not dare turn in without trying to get rid of the ice in the stovepipe. To start the thawing, I filled a soup can with meta tablets and played the flame up and down the sides of the pipe, thus supplying additional heat which the asbestos held. After the water started to run, the heat of the stove was enough to keep the flow going. Before it stopped, I collected a pail of water through the hole in the elbow crook. The thermograph trace was crossing 83° below zero, and the water was freezing on the floor as it struck. I hesitated to shut off the stove lest the instruments—not to mention myself—stop from the cold. I lay in the bag, thinking of warm, tropical places; doing this seemed to make me feel warmer. After a little while I got up and turned off the stove."

Alone *Richard E. Byrd (Putnam: London, 1938) pp. 262–265.*

Right: the leaders of the U.S. Navy's Operation Deep Freeze, making plans for the International Geophysical Year. On the left is Byrd who had earned the rank of Rear Admiral in the Navy and was the U.S. representative for the IGY.

The Explorers

AMUNDSEN, ROALD
1872–1928   Norway
1903–1906: Became first man to navigate the Northwest Passage.
1911: Commanded first party to successfully reach the South Pole.
1918–1920: Sailed through the Northeast Passage to the east.
1926: Flew over North Pole in dirigible, accompanied by Lincoln Elsworth and Umberto Nobile.
1928: Commanded rescue party to search for Umberto Nobile. Killed on this mission.
See maps on pages 87, 98

BAFFIN, WILLIAM
1584–1622   England
1612: Took part in an expedition to Greenland.
1615: Sailed with Robert Bylot in search of the Northwest Passage. Traveled through Hudson Strait into Hudson Bay. Gave his name to the large island on the northern side of Hudson Strait.
1616: Again with Bylot, made a second attempt to find the Northwest Passage. Explored Baffin Bay and discovered several sounds leading into the Arctic Ocean. These he named Jones, Smith, and Lancaster sounds.
See map on page 33

BARENTS, WILLEM
(?)–1597   The Netherlands
1594–1597: Chief pilot on three Dutch voyages to find Northeast Passage. Spent the winter of 1596–1597 on Novaya Zemlya with crew of third expedition. Died from exhaustion and perhaps scurvy on return journey south from Novaya Zemlya. Barents Sea named in his honor.
See map on page 33

BELLINGSHAUSEN, FABIAN (THADDEUS) VON
1778–1852   Estonia, Russia
1803: Took part in the first Russian circumnavigation of the world.
1819–1821: Sailed from Kronshtadt in the Baltic in command of the *Vostok* and the *Mirnyi*. Circumnavigated Antarctica and discovered Alexander I Island and Peter I Island, named for

the czars. Crossed Antarctic Circle at various points. Cruised in the Pacific during the winter months, resting at Sydney and visiting Tahiti and many other Pacific islands.
See map on page 51

BERING, VITUS
1680–1741   Denmark
1727–1729: Served in Russian Navy and commanded Russian sailing expedition along Siberian coast.
1740–1741: Commanded Russian expedition that landed on Kayak Island in Alaska. Died of scurvy on Bering Island. Bering Sea and Bering Strait named for him.
See map on page 33

BYRD, RICHARD EVELYN
1888–1957   United States
1926: With Floyd Bennett made first flight over North Pole.
1928–1930: Commanded U.S. expedition that established permanent base at Little America on Antarctica.
1929: With Bernt Balcon made first flight over South Pole.
1933–1935: Commanded U.S. scientific expedition to Antarctica.
1946–1947: Commanded Operation Highjump.
1955–1956: Organized establishment of Little America V.
1957: Commanded U.S. Antarctic program for IGY.
See map on page 154

CABOT, JOHN
1450–1498   Venice
1497: In the service of England, sailed west in search of Northwest Passage. Landed on either Newfoundland or Nova Scotia, and claimed the region for England. Returned home after sailing south and west around Cape Breton Island.
1498: Explored east and west coasts of Greenland. Followed the Labrador coast to Nova Scotia and then sailed southward, possibly even reaching Delaware Bay before starting back.

CHANCELLOR, RICHARD
(?)–1556   England
1553: Commanded the *Edward*

Bonaventure in voyage to find Northeast Passage. Visited Russian court at Moscow. Laid foundations of British trade with Russia.
See map on page 33

COOK, JAMES
1728–1779   England
1759: Surveyed and charted St. Lawrence Channel from Quebec to the sea.
1762–1767: Carried out surveys of the coast of Newfoundland and Labrador.
1768–1771: Commanded expedition for astronomical observations in the South Pacific. Landed at Tahiti, explored the Society Islands. Circumnavigated New Zealand and charted its coasts. Mapped the east coast of Australia. Proved that New Guinea was not joined to Australia.
1772–1775: Commanded the *Resolution* and the *Adventure* on a voyage designed to establish or disprove the existence of the Southern Continent. Crossed the Antarctic Circle and sailed back to New Zealand. Sailed south twice again but was driven back by ice. Visited Easter Island, the Marquesas Islands, the Society Islands, the Friendly Islands, the New Hebrides. Discovered New Caledonia and Norfolk Island. Surveyed Tierra del Fuego and South Georgia.
1778–1779: Commanded the *Resolution* and *Discovery* to search for the Northwest Passage from the Pacific to the Atlantic. Sailed to Tasmania, New Zealand, the Friendly and Society Islands. Revisited Tahiti. Discovered the Sandwich group, later renamed the Hawaiian Islands. Surveyed the Pacific coast of North America as far as Alaska. Passed through the Bering Strait and sailed northeast until stopped by ice. Returned to the Hawaiian Islands where he was killed on February 14, 1779.
See map on page 51

DAVIS, JOHN
1550(?)–1605   England
1585: First of three voyages to explore Northwest Passage. Pushed through strait named for him into Baffin Bay.

1586: Second voyage to Greenland, crossed Cumberland Sound, passed entrance to Hudson Bay and Hamilton Sound in Labrador.
1587: Sailed along west coast of Greenland to Hope Sanderson, then turned west and southward because he could not get through to the north.
1591–1593: During another search for Northwest Passage discovered the Falkland Islands.
1601: Sailed to Table Bay, around the Cape of Good Hope to Madagascar, Chagos Archipelago, Nicobar Islands, to the Moluccas. Returned to England.
See map on page 33

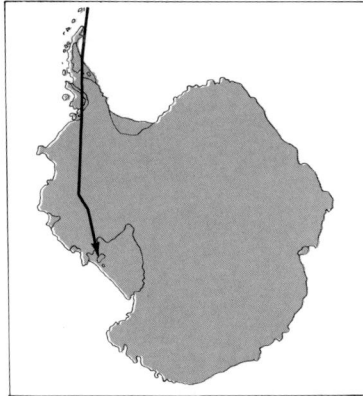

D'URVILLE, DUMONT JEAN
1780–1842   France
1822: He sailed with Duperrey to the Falkland Islands, went up the west coast of South America, then crossed the Pacific to New Ireland. He sailed to the Moluccas and around Australia, visiting southeastern Australia, New Zealand, the Carolines, and the East Indies.
1825–1829: Sailed to the Pacific again, crossing the Indian Ocean to Tasmania and visiting Santa Cruz Islands and the north coast of New Guinea. From here he again sailed around Australia.
1837–1840: He sailed around Cape Horn to Batavia and Tasmania. Then he discovered Adelie Land in Antarctica.
See map on page 51

ELLSWORTH, LINCOLN
1880–1951   United States

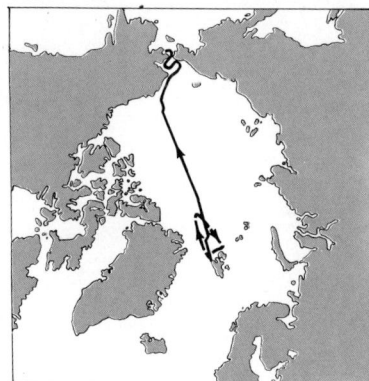

Worked as mining engineer in Alaska and served as field assistant with U.S. Biological Survey.
1924: Led a geological survey of Andes Mountains.
1925: With Roald Amundsen he made first aerial crossing of North Polar Basin.
1926: Co-leader of Amundsen-Ellsworth-Nobile Transpolar Flight.
1931: Participated in *Graf Zeppelin* dirigible flight to Arctic.
1935 and 1939: Made flights across Antarctica.

ERIC THE RED
900's   Norway
982: Left Iceland to spend three years exploring the west coast of Greenland before returning to the Icelandic community.
986: Sailed back to found colony centered at his homestead Brattahlid near present-day Julianehåb, Greenland.

FRANKLIN, SIR JOHN
1786–1847   England
1818: Accompanied by Sir George Back he made an attempt to get to the north of Spitzbergen.
1819–1821: Accompanied by Back, he sailed into Hudson Bay and went overland to the Great Slave Lake and down the Coppermine River to the mouth, then westward for 500 miles to Cape Turnagain.
1825: Traveled down the Mackenzie River to the mouth, then westward for 370 miles to Point Barrow.
1845-1847: He sailed into Lancaster Sound and sailed south between Somerset Island and Prince of Wales Island. Somewhere there his ships were frozen in. The expedition tried to journey southward but all men perished.
See map on pages 62–63

FROBISHER, SIR MARTIN
1535(?)–1594   England
1576: First voyage to find Northwest Passage. Discovered Frobisher Bay on Baffin Island.
1577: Second voyage to Northwest Passage. Claimed Greenland for Queen Elizabeth I.
1578: Commanded third expedition, which ended in failure. Knighted for fighting against the Spanish Armada.
See map on page 33

FUCHS, SIR VIVIAN ERNEST
born 1908   England
1929: Went with the "Cambridge East Greenland Expedition" as geologist.
1930: Went on a Cambridge expedition to the East African lakes.
1931: Went on an archaeological expedition to East Africa.
1933: Explored Lake Rudolf in the Rift Valley.
1937: Went to Lake Rukwa in East Africa.
1947–1950: Led Falkland Islands Dependencies Survey in Antarctica.
1950: Director of the Falkland Island Dependencies Survey.
1957–1958: Commanded British Commonwealth Trans-Antarctic Expedition. Crossed Antarctica in 99 days and covered 2,158 miles.
See map on page 154

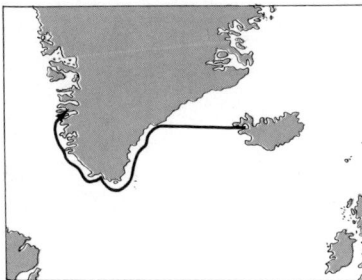

HALL, CHARLES FRANCIS

1821–1871   United States
1860–1862: Led Arctic expedition.
1864–1869: Set off to look for missing Franklin men.
1871: Commanded U.S. expedition to find North Pole. Sledged to northern limits of Greenland Ice Sheet and discovered Hall Land. Crossed Kennedy Channel and traveled up East Coast of Ellesmere Island. Died from poisoning on returning to his ship the *Polaris*.

HERBERT, WALLY

born 1934   England
Mid 1940s: Served as surveyor in the Antarctic; traveled with dog teams down central plateau of Graham Land.
1960: Joined expedition to Lapland and Spitzbergen.
1960–1962: Led Southern Party that mapped unexplored country between Beardmore Glacier and the Axel Heiberg Glacier.
1968–1969: Commanded British Trans-Arctic Expedition, the first surface crossing of the Arctic Ocean.
See map on page 87

HILLARY, SIR EDMUND PERCIVAL

born 1919   New Zealand
1939: Mountaineer who began climbing in New Zealand.
1953: Member of the British expedition to Mount Everest. With Tenzing Norgay was first to reach the summit.
1957: With Vivian Fuchs made possible the first land crossing of Antarctica. Hillary's party established supply depots from the Ross Sea to the South Pole.
See map on page 154

HUDSON, HENRY

(?)–1611   England
1607: In the service of the English Muscovy Company, sought a North-east Passage to the Orient.
1608: Sailed northeast again, this time reaching Novaya Zemlya.
1609: Sailed to North America in the service of the Dutch East India Company. Entered New York harbor and explored the Hudson River northward to present-day Albany.
1610–1611: In the service of England, sailed west in search of the Northwest Passage. Discovered Hudson Strait and Hudson Bay. Was cast adrift by his mutinous crew in James Bay.
See map on page 33

MAWSON, SIR DOUGLAS

1882–1958   England
(Went to Australia when a boy.)
1907–1909: Went to the Ross Barrier and to the South Magnetic Pole with the Shackleton expedition.
1911–1914: Explored the area between Kaiser Wilhelm II Land and Victoria Land in the Antarctic. He discovered George V and Queen Mary Lands.
1929–1931: During his third Antarctic expedition discovered MacRobertson Land, and sailed along the edge of the continent for several hundred miles.
See map on pages 98–99

McCLINTOCK, SIR FRANCIS LEOPOLD

1819–1907   England
1848–1849: Sailed on Franklin search mission under Sir James Clark Ross.
1850–1851; 1852–1854: Made two further Arctic voyages during which he perfected sledging methods and equipment for Arctic journeys.
1857–1859: Commissioned by Lady Franklin to command expedition aboard the *Fox*, which was to sail to King William Island. Found message and remains on King William Island that explained fate of Franklin expedition.
See map on pages 62–63

NANSEN, FRIDTJOF

1861–1930   Norway
1888: Crossed Greenland in the summer with five other men.
1893: On June 24 sailed in the *Fram* to drift over the polar icecap. With Hjalmar Johansen tried to reach North Pole with kayaks and sledges. Came to within 272 miles of the pole.
1896: Returned to Norway in August.
1906–1908: Norwegian minister to Great Britain.
1914–1918: World War I work with prisoners of war.
1922: Received Nobel Peace Prize.
See map on page 87

NORDENSKJÖLD, NILS ADOLF ERIK

1832–1901   Finland
1857: Moved to Sweden and became Swedish citizen.
1868: Led north polar expedition that reached to within 400 nautical miles of the pole.
1870: Studied geology of Greenland.
1878–1879: First man to sail through Northeast Passage.
1883: Traveled over inland icecap of Greenland.
See map foot of previous column

PALMER, NATHANIEL BROWN

1799–1877   United States
Believed to be the first explorer to sight what is now called the Antarctic Peninsula. Discovered Deception Island.

PARRY, SIR WILLIAM EDWARD

1790–1855   England
1818: With John Ross and J. C. Ross, he sailed to Baffin Bay and Lancaster Sound.
1819–1820: With J. C. Ross, he sailed through Lancaster Sound to Melville Island and reached 110°W.
1821–1823: Again with J. C. Ross, he discovered Fury and Hecla Strait.
1824–1825: Still with Ross, he went to Lancaster Sound, Prince Regent Inlet, but failed to get through.
1827: Tried to reach the North Pole from Spitzbergen. Came to within 500 miles of the pole.
See map on page 33

PEARY, ROBERT EDWIN

1856–1920   United States
1884–1888: Worked as surveyor for U.S. Navy on Nicaraguan Canal.
1886: Made first trip to Greenland.
1893–1897: Made frequent expeditions to Greenland and regions adjacent.
1897–1901: Four-year expedition to reach the North Pole.
1905: Commanded first North Pole expedition aboard U.S.S. *Roosevelt*.
1908: Commanded second polar expedition aboard the *Roosevelt*.
1909: On April 6 became first explorer to reach the North Pole.
See map on page 87

PYTHEAS

about 325 B.C.   Greece
Sailed from Massalia the Greek colony where he was born, (now Marseille, France). Rounded Iberian Peninsula and sailed north to British Isles and explored them. Sailed from Shetland and Orkney Islands into Arctic Sea. He may have reached Thule (Norway or Iceland). He made scientific observations during the voyage, one being of the midnight sun.
See map top of next column

RAE, JOHN
1813–1893   Scotland
Resident surgeon at Hudson's Bay
Company station at Moose Factory.
Discovered evidence of missing
Franklin men.
1846: Made expedition to Repulse Bay
and surveyed 700 miles of coastline.
1851: Traveled and mapped 700 miles
of new coast on south side of Wollaston
Peninsula on Victoria Island.
1853–1854: Commanded expedition
that obtained news of fate of lost
Franklin mission from Eskimos on
Boothia Peninsula.
See map on pages 62–63

ROSS, SIR JAMES CLARK
1800–1862   England
1818: With his uncle John Ross he
sailed to Baffin Bay and Lancaster
Sound.
1819–1820; With Parry, he sailed
through Lancaster Sound and Barrow
Strait. They went westward along
630 miles of coast to Melville Island.
1821–1823: Still with Parry, he went to
Lancaster Sound but was shipwrecked.
1829–1833: With his uncle, he reached
King William Island.
1840–1843: Sailed to the Antarctic and
into the Ross Sea, discovering Mount
Erebus and Mount Terror. After
cruising around the Ross Sea to
74° 20′ S., he set course for Tasmania,
where he wintered. The second part
of the voyage took him 1400 miles
farther east to 78° 10′ S. The third part
took him into the Weddell Sea area.
1848: Sailed to the Canadian Arctic in

search of Franklin.
See map on page 51

ROSS, SIR JOHN
1777–1856   Scotland
1818: Accompanied by his nephew, he
sailed from England up Baffin Bay,
touching Ellesmere Land and Devon
Island. He went part way into Lancaster
Sound, then went down the east coast
of Baffin Island.
1829–1833: Sailed again to the Canadian Arctic with his nephew, this time
going through Lancaster Sound and
Prince Regent Inlet to the Gulf of
Boothia. They traveled overland across
the Boothia Peninsula to King William
Island.
1850–1851: Sailed with his nephew to
the Canadian Arctic in search of
Franklin.
See maps on pages 33, 62–63

SCOTT, ROBERT FALCON
1868–1912   England
1901–1904: Member of first expedition
to reach south polar plateau.
1910: Sailed from New Zealand in
command of South Pole expedition.
1911: In November started over the
ice to South Pole.
1912: With four other men reached the
pole on January 18. Died from hunger
and cold on the return journey.
See map on pages 98–99

SHACKLETON, SIR ERNEST HENRY
1875–1922   Ireland
1901–1904: With Scott's expedition he
coasted the Ross Barrier and discovered
King Edward VII Land. From the south
of Ross Island, he sledged overland to
82° 17′ S.
1907–1909: With Mawson he landed
at Cape Royds on Ross Island in
McMurdo Sound. Attempted to reach
the South Pole by way of the Beardmore Glacier. He reached 88° 23′ S.—
97 miles from the pole.
1914: Commanded British Trans-
Antarctic Expedition. Ice in the Weddell
Sea crushed the expedition ship called
the Endurance. Safely evacuated members of expedition to Elephant Island.
With five other men he sailed in small
boat to South Georgia Island. Crossed
South Georgia Island to alert rescuers.
With help he returned to Elephant
Island and rescued rest of his party.
See map on pages 98–99

STEFANSSON, VILHJALMUR
1879–1962   Canada
1906–1907: Led anthropological
expedition to study Eskimos of
Mackenzie River Delta.
1908–1912: Second expedition to
Mackenzie Delta. Visited Victoria
Island Eskimos. Returned to San

Francisco via Point Barrow.
1913–1918: Led Canadian Arctic
expedition to explore Canadian and
Alaskan regions of the Arctic.
See map on page 128

WEDDELL, JAMES
1787–1834   England
1819–1820: Sailed to the South
Shetland Islands.
1822–1823: Reached the South
Orkney Islands; then went farther
south to 74° 15′ S., 34° 16′ W.
See map on page 51

WILKES, CHARLES
1798–1877   United States
1834–1842: Commanded first U.S.
expedition to Antarctica. Wilkes Land
on Antarctic continent named in his
honor.
1861: As commander of the San Jacinto
during American Civil War captured
Confederate commissioners sailing
aboard British mail steamer. Later sent
to command squadron in West Indies.
1844–1861: Engaged in preparing
reports of expedition. Of the 28 volumes
planned only 19 were published.
See map on page 51

WILKINS, SIR HUBERT
1888–1958   Australia
1919: Navigated pioneering airplane
flight from Britain to Australia.
1920 and 1921: Participated in two
British Antarctic expeditions.
1928: With Carl B. Eielson flew
airplane over Arctic Ocean from Point
Barrow, Alaska to Spitzbergen.
1931: Tried to reach North Pole by
submarine.
1933–1939: Managed Lincoln
Ellsworth's Antarctic expeditions.
1942–1945: Served in U.S. Department
of War and Defense.
See map on page 154

Glossary

Antarctic Circle: An imaginary circle that runs parallel to the equator. It marks off the South Frigid Zone from the South Temperate Zone.

anthropology: The scientific study of man. An anthropologist studies where the races of man originated, how they live, the languages they speak, and their ways of working, eating, courting, and worshiping.

Arctic Circle: An imaginary line marking off the Arctic region from the North Temperate Zone. It runs through the northern parts of Russia, Scandinavia, Greenland, Canada, Alaska, and the northern tip of Iceland.

caribou: The French-Canadian name for the wild reindeer of North America. The Northern Indians and Eskimos depend on the caribou. They eat its flesh and make soup from its marrow, and clothing and tents from its hide. They use its bones for needles and knives; its horns for fishhooks, spears, and spoons; and its tendons for thread.

continental glacier: A large body of ice or an icecap such as that covering Antarctica. It covers an area larger than the United States and is 8,000 feet thick at the South Pole. The next largest continental glacier is the Greenland Icecap.

crevasse: A deep crack in an earth embankment or a glacier. Huge crevasses are common on all glaciers and make it dangerous or even impossible to cross them.

Dew Line or Distant Early Warning Line: A line of radar stations that protects the United States and Canada against air attack from the north. There are 64 stations in this line, which extends 4,500 miles from the Aleutian Islands across Canada to Iceland.

Eskimo: The hardy people who live in the cold, arctic regions of North America and northeastern Asia are called *Eskimos*. Their homeland stretches from Siberia across Alaska and Canada to Greenland. The word *Eskimo* means "eaters of raw meat." Northern Indians gave them this name because Eskimos often do not cook their food. Like the American Indians, Eskimos belong to the Mongoloid stock. They have straight black hair, dark brown eyes, high cheekbones, and wide faces. But Eskimos are not Indians. They have shorter arms and legs, smaller hands and feet, and lighter skins than Indians. The ancestors of the Eskimos probably came from Asia by boat more than 6,000 years ago. Their way of life developed in the region that is now Alaska. Many generations of Eskimos spread over the land. They reached Greenland more than 1,000 years ago.

frostbite: The effect of extreme cold on the body. Frostbite usually affects the ears, nose, hands, and feet. Early symptoms of frostbite include tingling, numbness, and pain. Sometimes in severe cases the skin on the frostbitten area blisters and peels off as in the case of sunburn.

Greenwich Meridian: The prime meridian of the earth that passes through Greenwich, a borough of London, England. It is located on 0° longitude, and all other meridians of longitude are numbered east or west of the prime meridian.

iceberg: A huge mass of ice that breaks off the lower end of a glacier and falls into the sea. The biggest icebergs rise as much as 400 feet above the surface of the ocean. But only from one-eighth to one-tenth of the total mass of the iceberg is above the water. North Atlantic icebergs come from Greenland. In the Antarctic region enormous icebergs drift out to sea from the Antarctic icecap.

icecap: One of the thick layers of ice and snow that covers large areas of land in the polar regions. The Antarctic icecap covers more than 5 million square miles, an area greater than the United States, Mexico, and Central America put together. The thickness of this icecap varies from 1,000 feet near the coast to 6,000 feet in the interior. Most of Greenland is also covered by an icecap.

igloo: The Eskimo name for a shelter, such as a tent of canvas or animal skins, or a house made of snow, sod, or stone. The best-known igloo is the winter snowhouse of the Central Canadian Eskimos, made of hard-packed snow cut into blocks. These blocks are fitted together in a spiral that becomes smaller at the top to form a dome. The igloo is heated by a lamp that burns blubber or seal oil. Entry into an igloo is by a passage tunneled under the snow. Thus cold air cannot blow into the igloo and the warm air inside collects under the dome.

International Date Line: A voyager traveling eastward to the opposite side of the globe will be 12 hours in advance of the sun; one traveling westward, 12 hours behind the sun. To prevent confusion, the 180th meridian was chosen as a convenient point (the International Date Line) at which the date could be altered – forward if traveling west, backward if going east.

International Geophysical Year (IGY): The period between July 1, 1957, and December 31, 1958, when scientists from 66 countries worked together to investigate various aspects of the earth and its surroundings. Much emphasis was put on scientific observations in the polar regions. Twelve countries established more than 30 scientific bases in Antarctica. After the IGY ended, most of the countries that had taken part in the Antarctic program continued scientific research there and formed an international organization called the Special Committee for Antarctic Research (SCAR).

Lapps: The people who live in the extreme northern part of Europe above the Arctic Circle. The region is called Lapland and stretches across the northern parts of Norway, Sweden,

Finland, and Russia. They are mostly nomadic people who follow the reindeer herds. Some live as fishermen and farmers on the Atlantic and Arctic coasts.

latitude: The position north or south of a point on the surface of the earth relative to the equator. The equator has a latitude of 0°, the North Pole 90° north, and the South Pole 90° south.

longitude: A measure of east and west distance. Degrees of longitude are counted east and west of a line running through Greenwich, England, which most countries in the world have agreed is 0° longitude. The globe is divided by a series of lines running north and south so that there are 360 equal parts. Lines of longitude, together with lines of latitude, help us to plot our position on the globe. Longitude also helps us to know the time in other places, since an hour of time equals 15° of longitude. Therefore when it is noon in Greenwich (0°) it is 7 A.M. in New York City (74° west).

magnetic poles: The two small constantly moving regions located in the north and south polar areas, toward which the compass needle points from any direction throughout adjacent regions. In 1960 the North Magnetic Pole was sited about 1000 miles from the North Geographic Pole, near Bathurst Island in northern Canada. The south Magnetic Pole in 1960 was about 1600 miles from the South Geographic Pole, and located near the Adelie Land Coast of Antarctica.

midnight sun: The sun shines at midnight at certain times of the year in the polar regions. At the Arctic Circle this occurs on June 22. Farther north, the periods of midnight sun last longer. For example, in northern Norway, there is continuous daylight from May through July. At the North Pole, the sun does not set for six months from about March 21 to September 21. At the Antarctic Circle 24 hours of sunlight occurs on December 21, and the South Pole has midnight sun between

September 21 and March 21. The midnight sun is caused by the tilting of the earth toward the sun. As the earth travels around the sun, first the South Pole and then the North Pole face the sun.

meridian: The line on a globe or map that shows the distance east or west of the prime meridian at Greenwich, England. Sailors and pilots use meridians to find out the positions of their ships or airplanes.

narwhal: An unusual whale of the Arctic. The male has a spiral ivory tusk about eight feet long jutting out of the left side of its head. The tusk is really the narwhal's only tooth. A few narwhals, mostly females, have two tusks. The Eskimos of Greenland hunt narwhals and make tools out of the ivory tusks.

Operation Deep Freeze: The operations engaged in by the U.S. Navy in preparation for IGY. During 1955, the navy, under the command of Rear Admiral Richard Byrd, established bases around Antarctica.

pemmican: Dried meat pounded into a powder and mixed with hot fat and sometimes dried fruits or berries. This mixture is pressed into a loaf or cakes that can be easily carried. Pemmican was a staple item in the diet of the polar explorers who had to reduce to a minimum the weight of the supplies they loaded on to their sledges.

polar ice pack: The masses of broken, piled-up ice that cover most of the Arctic Ocean. In summer, the combination of rising temperatures, tides, and wind break up the pack into floes.

Ross Ice Shelf: An ice barrier that fills the southern part of the Ross Sea. At the edge of the shelf icy cliffs rise from 850 feet below the water to 150 feet above the surface.

scurvy: A disease caused by a lack of vitamin C in the diet. It was once a

common affliction among sailors and polar explorers in particular. If a person does not get enough vitamin C, any wound he might have heals poorly, his gums begin to bleed and his teeth become loose. The person's joints become sore, he loses his appetite and becomes restless. Food containing vitamin C, such as citrus fruits, tomatoes, raw cabbage, lettuce, celery, onions, carrots, and potatoes – eaten fresh – can prevent and sometimes help to cure scurvy.

Stone Age: The term used to designate the period in all human cultures when men used stone rather than metal tools. Scientists divide the Stone Age on the basis of tool-making techniques into three periods: the Paleolithic (from more than $1\frac{1}{2}$ million years ago to 8000 B.C.); the Mesolithic (from 8000 B.C. to 7000 B.C.); the Neolithic (from about 7000 B.C. up to the invention of metals). Many people were still in the Stone Age when they were first discovered by European explorers – for instance, the American Indians.

tundra: The low, swampy plains that lie around the Arctic Ocean in northern Europe, Siberia, North America, and a few areas of the Southern Hemisphere. The ground is perpetually frozen to a great depth except for a few feet at the surface that thaw in summer. The tundra occupies a tenth of the earth's land surface and separates the sea and the ice of the Arctic from the forests.

Index

Picture Credits

Listed below are the sources of all the illustrations in this book. To identify the source of a particular illustration, first find the relevant page on the diagram opposite. The number in black in the appropriate position on that page refers to the credit as listed below.

1 Aldus Archives
2 Photo Carmelo Guadagno, courtesy American Geographical Society
3 H. Aschehoug & Co., Oslo
4 Baumkotter Antiques/Photo John Webb © Aldus Books
5 Bibliothèque Nationale, Paris/Photo Denise Bourbonnais © Aldus Books
6 Emil Schulthess/Black Star, London
7 By permission of the Curators of the Bodleian Library
8 Collection André Breton, Paris/Michael Holford Library
9 Reproduced by permission of the Trustees of the British Museum
10 British Museum/Photo R.B. Fleming © Aldus Books
11 British Museum/Michael Holford Library
12 British Museum, courtesy Peter Scott
13 British Museum (Natural History)/ Photo John Webb © Aldus Books
14 Collection Count Brobinskoy/ Michael Holford Library
15 Brown Brothers
16 Courtesy Cavalry Club, London
17 Central Office and Museum of National Antiquities, Stockholm/ Photo S. Hallgren
18 Reproduced from *Farthest North,* Constable & Co. Ltd., London, 1897
19 Fram Museum/Photo Mittet
20 Geographical Projects Limited, London
21 Dr. Georg Gerster
22 Courtesy of John Hancock Mutual Life Insurance Company, Boston, Mass.
23 Wally Herbert/British Trans-Arctic Expedition
24 Wally Herbert/Topix
25 Photo Chauncey C. Loomis
26 The Mansell Collection
27 Photo Jeremy Whitaker © Aldus Books, courtesy Lord Middleton
28 Ministère de la Guerre, Paris/Photo Giraudon © S.P.A.D.E.M.
29 The Mitchell Library, Sydney, New South Wales/Photo Brian Bird
30 Musée Arts Africains et Océaniens, Paris/Photo Giraudon © S.P.A.D.E.M.
31 Reference Collection, Center for Polar Archives, National Archives, Washington, D.C.
32 Records of the United States Information Agency, Audiovisual Branch, National Archives, Washington, D.C.
33 Courtesy of National Collection of Fine Arts, Smithsonian Institution
34 © National Geographic Society, Courtesy Robert E. Peary Jr. and Marie Peary Kuhne
35 National Maritime Museum, Greenwich/Photo Michael Holford © Aldus Books
36 National Maritime Museum, Greenwich/Photo John Webb © Aldus Books
37 National Portrait Gallery, London
38 National Portrait Gallery, Smithsonian Institution, Washington, D.C.
39 © Nationalmuseum, Copenhagen
40 Novosti
41 Oslo Bymuseum
42 By kind permission of The Parker Gallery, London
43 Peabody Museum, Harvard University
44 Pitt-Rivers Museum, University of Oxford
45 Popperfoto
46 Public Archives of Canada
47 Courtesy Queen Victoria Museum and Art Gallery, Launceston, Tasmania
48 By kind permission of Mrs. P.E. Quick
49 Rijksmuseum, Amsterdam
50 Reproduced by permission of the Royal Geographical Society
51 Photo John Webb © Aldus Books, reproduced by permission of the Royal Geographical Society
52 Emil Schulthess
53 Scott Polar Research Institute, Cambridge, England
54 Photo John Webb © Aldus Books, courtesy Scott Polar Research Institute, Cambridge, England
55 *Stern* Archiv
56 *Sunday Times* Colour Magazine
57 Charles Swithinbank
58 Trans-Antarctic Expedition Committee
59 Victoria & Albert Museum, London/Photo John Webb © Aldus Books
60 The Beinecke Rare Book and Manuscript Library, Yale University, courtesy of American Heritage

Pages	Contents
TITLEPAGE	13
4–5	21
6–7	20, 20
8–9	56, 34
10–11	57, 9
12–13	17, 57
14–15	39, 9
16–17	28, 59
18–19	57, 52
20–21	10, 27
22–23	10, 7, 10
24–25	10, 10, 49
26–27	9, 14
28–29	10, 44
30–31	37, 37, 54
32–33	20
34–35	54, 54
36–37	9, 29
38–39	13, 54
40–41	2, 1, 50, 40
42–43	5, 4, 30
44–45	5, 42, 5
46–47	38, 60, 50
48–49	54, 54
50–51	6, 20
52–53	35
54–55	35, 36
56–57	37, 47, 42
58–59	26, 37, 35
60–61	35, 26, 37, 35
62–63	26, 20
64–65	26, 35
66–67	35, 1
68–69	18, 3
70–71	26, 19, 19, 3
72–73	3, 3
74–75	20, 3, 3
76–77	3, 3, 3, 3
78–79	3, 3
80–81	34, 15
82–83	34, 56, 15
84–85	33, 33, 34
86–87	22, 20
88–89	9, 34
90–91	19, 45
92–93	45, 45, 19
94–95	45, 12, 21
96–97	45, 45, 53
98–99	26, 20
100–101	45, 53
102–103	45, 45
104–105	53, 16
106–107	48, 12, 57
108–109	26, 21, 1
110–111	57, 26, 1
112–113	57, 1
114–115	26, 51
116–117	50, 1
118–119	15, 4
120–121	43, 54
122–123	10, 10, 1
124–125	1, 43
126–127	46, 43
128–129	1, 20
130–131	9, 42, 8
132–133	11, 15
134–135	51, 51
136–137	50, 35, 50
138–139	50, 21
140–141	50, 51
142–143	50, 50
144–145	21
146–147	15, 57, 15
148–149	32, 52
150–151	52, 58
152–153	52
154–155	20, 52, 57
156–157	41, 55, 55
158–159	56, 56, 57
160–161	21, 1
162–163	49, 1, 1
164–165	31, 31, 26, 25
166–167	1, 18, 1, 1
168–169	15, 15, 26
170–171	15, 24, 24
172–173	23, 24, 23
174–175	46, 1, 43
176–177	45, 45, 45
178–179	45, 15, 45
180–181	32, 15, 15
182–183	
184–185	
186–187	
188–189	
190–191	
192	